# customizing
# windows xp

## Visual QuickProject Guide

by John Rizzo

Peachpit
Press

Visual QuickProject Guide
# Customizing Windows XP
John Rizzo

## Peachpit Press
1249 Eighth Street
Berkeley, CA 94710
510/524-2178
800/283-9444
510/524-2221 (fax)

Find us on the World Wide Web at: www.peachpit.com
To report errors, please send a note to errata@peachpit.com
Peachpit Press is a division of Pearson Education

Copyright © 2005 by John Rizzo

Editor: Suzie Lowey Nasol
Production Editor: Lupe Edgar
Compositor: Owen Wolfson
Indexer: FireCrystal Communications
Cover design: The Visual Group with Aren Howell
Interior design: Elizabeth Castro Cover
Photo credit: PhotoDisc

ISBN 0-321-32124-3

9 8 7 6 5 4 3 2 1

Printed and bound in the United States of America

## Special Thanks to...

Christine for her continuing support and tolerance of my work habits;

Sal for his patience and persistence and for his continuing interest in my work;

Suzie Lowey Nasol for being at the helm and adeptly steering this project's journey to a successful conclusion;

Cliff Colby for pointing me towards this project;

and to the folks at Peachpit Press for their superb design and production values, and for throwing a great party in a 100-year-old San Francisco bar.

# contents

# contents

# contents

# introduction

The Visual QuickProject Guide you're reading offers a unique way to learn new skills. Instead of drowning you in long text descriptions, this Visual QuickProject Guide uses color screen shots with clear, concise, step-by-step instructions to show you how to complete a customization project in a matter of minutes.

The projects in this book personalize different aspects of Windows XP, so that your computer looks and acts the way that best fits your personal style of working. We'll dig into some of the many configuration dialog boxes to expose the plethora of options available to you. In fact, one problem confronting many people is the fact that Windows XP offers so many options that it can become overwhelming. To narrow it down, we'll focus in on the settings that make Windows XP more intuitive and useful. You may not care for every customization feature presented in this book, but by following along with each project, you'll learn some of the possibilities Windows XP offers. Once you see how configuration works, you'll be able to continue to explore the other customization options available to you.

We will be working with the standard settings dialog boxes to make changes to a variety of different parts of Windows, including the Desktop and Start menu, files, folders and windows, and the way you work with the Internet.

# what you'll learn

Personalize the Desktop with your own art and make other modifications.

Add different types of toolbars to the edges of your screen.

Create shortcuts to files and dialog boxes.

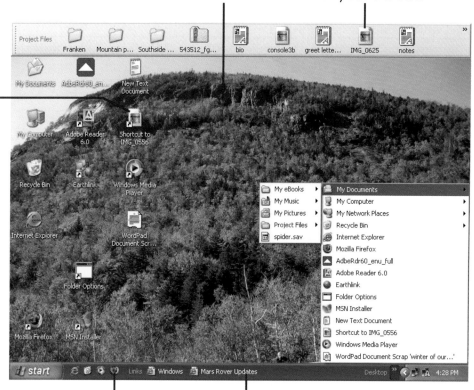

Add your own programs to the Quicklaunch area of the toolbar.

Add toolbars to the Taskbar for access to the Internet, your files, and other Windows XP features.

Replace Internet Explorer with another Program as your default Web browser.

Change static icons into hierarchical menus.

Add your programs and folders to the top of the Start menu.

Change the number of recently used program icons displayed.

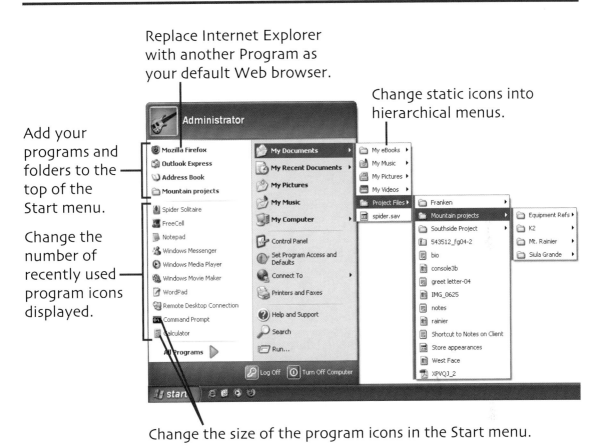

Change the size of the program icons in the Start menu.

# what you'll learn (cont.)

Add new icons to the window toolbar.

Hide or display the side pane.

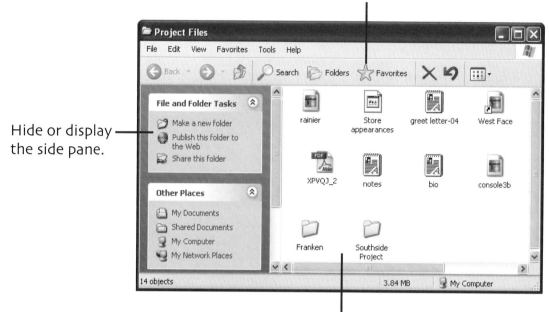

Use custom icons for files and folders.

Automatically arrange file icons in different ways.

Hide or display various window toolbars.

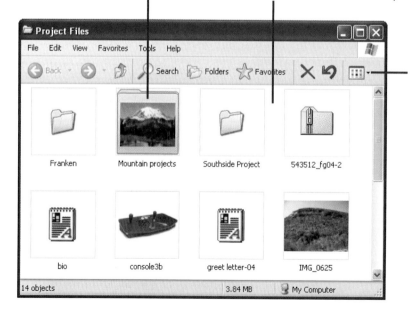

Add new software and remove old software.

Add new Windows features and update Windows.

Change the default programs that open certain types of files.

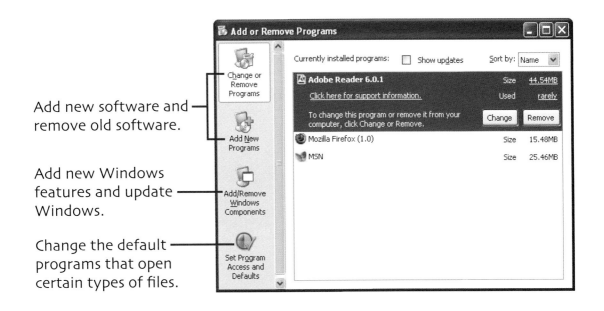

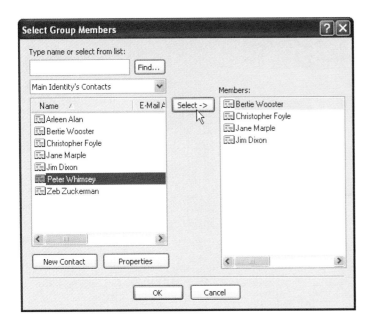

Create a high-speed Internet connection, turn off Outlook Express graphics to keep spammers at bay, and create groups in Outlook Express' address book.

# how this book works

The title of each section explains what is covered on that page.

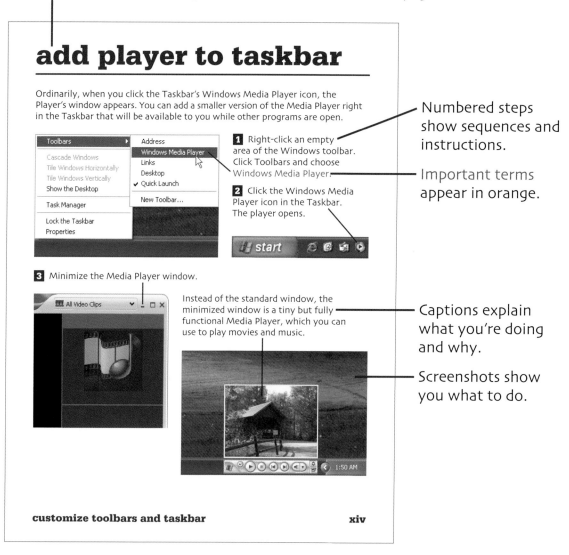

## add player to taskbar

Ordinarily, when you click the Taskbar's Windows Media Player icon, the Player's window appears. You can add a smaller version of the Media Player right in the Taskbar that will be available to you while other programs are open.

**1** Right-click an empty area of the Windows toolbar. Click Toolbars and choose Windows Media Player.

**2** Click the Windows Media Player icon in the Taskbar. The player opens.

**3** Minimize the Media Player window.

Instead of the standard window, the minimized window is a tiny but fully functional Media Player, which you can use to play movies and music.

— Numbered steps show sequences and instructions.

— Important terms appear in orange.

— Captions explain what you're doing and why.

— Screenshots show you what to do.

**customize toolbars and taskbar**                    xiv

The extra bits section at the end of each chapter contains additional tips and tricks that you might like to know—but that aren't absolutely necessary.

# extra bits

The heading for each group of tips matches the section title.

The page number next to the heading makes it easy to refer back to the main content.

## place files and folders p. 48

- Did you know that the documents and shortcut files on the Desktop actually sit inside a folder called, well, Desktop?

  It's in the Documents and Settings folder, inside a folder named after your user name.

  Add an item to the Desktop folder and it appears on the Desktop.

- Have you ever wanted easy access to a small portion of a file? You don't have to create a new document—just create a scrap.

  To create a scrap, simply select some text—a paragraph, sentence, or phrase—and drag it from the document window to the Desktop. A new file is created that has an icon with a jagged bottom.

## cleanup desktop p. 52

- Another way to quickly access your Desktop icons is with a key command. You can press Windows-D to minimize all of the open windows at the same time.

  This technique will even minimize windows that don't have a minimize button, such as dialog boxes and the Control Panel.

  Pressing Windows-D again will restore all of the windows you just minimized—unless you've opened, minimized, or restored any windows since hitting the command. If that's the case, Windows-D will only work on the last window you worked with.

**rearrange desktop items**

**introduction**

# the next step

While this Visual QuickProject Guide will give you a foundation in customizing the way your computer looks and acts, there's much more to learn about Windows XP.

If you want to dive into the details of using and configuring Windows XP, try Windows XP: Visual QuickStart Guide, also published by Peachpit Press, as an in-depth, handy reference.

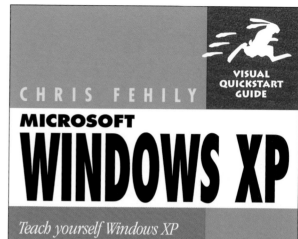

The Windows XP VQS features clear examples, concise, step-by-step instructions, hundreds of illustrations, and lots of helpful tips that will help you master Windows XP.

## Chapter 11

## Organizing Your Clips

After capturing or importing clips, you can organize them in *collections*—Explorer-like folder hierarchies (**Figure 11.5**). A collection doesn't apply to any specific movie project; you can use it many times over in different movies.

**To create a collection:**

1. If the Collections pane is hidden, choose View > Collections.

2. In the Collections pane, right-click the collection folder where you want to add your new collection; then choose New Collection (refer to Figure 11.5).

3. Type a name for the collection; then press Enter.

✔ **Tips**

■ Right-click a collection to rename or delete it. Deleting a collection or clip deletes only pointers; source files remain in their original locations on your hard drive.

■ Collections are stored as .dat files in the hidden folder \Documents and Settings\ *<user_name>*\Local Settings\Application Data\Microsoft\Movie Maker. Again, backing up a collection file doesn't back up the source files.

To store a clip in a particular collection folder, just drag the clip's icon from the Contents pane to the folder. You can sort the clips in the Contents pane.

**To arrange clips:**

1. In the Collections pane, click the collection folder that contains the clips that you want to arrange.
   The clips appear in the Contents pane.

2. To change how much detail is displayed, choose View > Details or View > Thumbnails.

3. Choose View > Arrange Icons By; then choose a property to display (**Figure 11.6**).

296

**Figure 11.5** Here's a reasonable way to organize clips in a collection hierarchy. Alternatively, you can organize your clips by event, rather than by clip type. If you have only a few clips, you can stick them all in one collection folder.

**Figure 11.6** You also can arrange clips via the shortcut menu; just right-click an empty area of the Contents pane.

# 1. explore windows xp customization

Where do I start?

That's the first question that comes to mind when seeking to personalize Windows XP. The answer can be found all over Windows. You can start with shortcut menus, the Start menu, the taskbar and toolbars, and other menus.

Your destination can be a properties dialog box, items in the Control Panel, or other dialog boxes. There are often different ways to get to a particular settings dialog box which may have buttons and tabs to get where you need to be, and other times Windows will launch wizards to guide you through a set up process.

# open shortcut menus

In Windows XP, pressing the right mouse button (known as right-clicking) will open a menu known as a shortcut menu. Many customizations in this book begin by bringing up a shortcut menu.

Not all shortcut menus are the same, however. What the shortcut menu looks like depends on what the cursor is pointing to when you right-click.

Try right-clicking on different objects: files, the Taskbar, items in the Start menu, title bars of windows, and even empty space on the Desktop. The shortcut menu that appears will have options specific to the object you are pointing to.

Shortcut menus present options that you can also get to from various menus and toolbars throughout Windows. The shortcut menu is usually the quickest way to access these options.

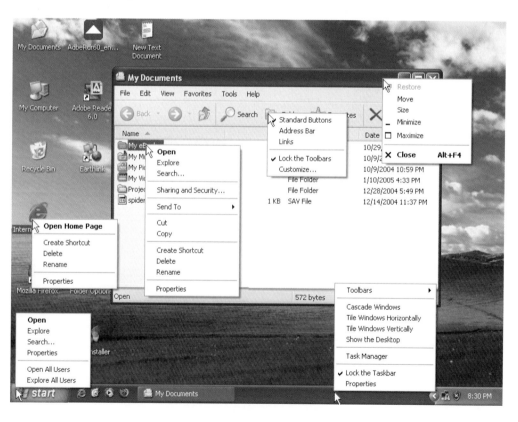

# properties windows

Many of the shortcut menus contain a Properties command. This brings up a properties dialog box that has settings specific to the item you right-clicked.

Much of the personalizing you'll do in Windows XP will take place in these properties dialog boxes, which are as varied as shortcut menus. Some, such as file properties dialog boxes, are simple, offering only a few settings options.

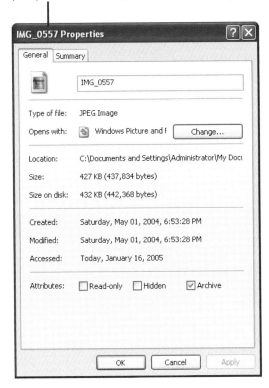

Others are more complex, with multiple tabs, each containing numerous settings options.

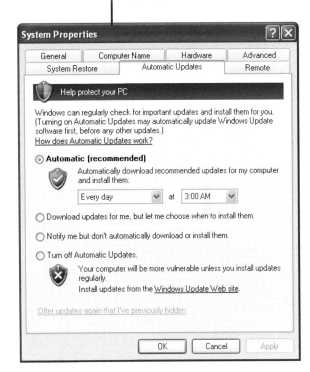

# use the control panel

The Control Panel is a repository for all kinds of settings dialog boxes. If you're not sure where to find certain properties dialog boxes or other settings, you can click around in the Control Panel. The Control Panel is also handy if you're accessing multiple settings dialog boxes.

There are two main ways to view the Control Panel. The default is the category view, which displays icons that represent categories of settings dialog boxes. Click an icon here and you'll be presented with a number of choices.

You can get to the Control Panel from the Start menu.

If you know what you're looking for, try clicking Switch to Classic View.

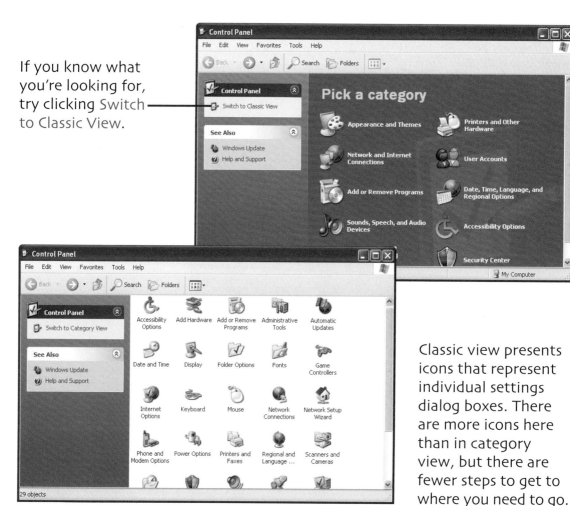

Classic view presents icons that represent individual settings dialog boxes. There are more icons here than in category view, but there are fewer steps to get to where you need to go.

# run wizards

A wizard is a program that gives you step-by-step instructions for setting up a specific feature. Windows XP contains dozens of wizards that guide you through tasks such as creating an Internet connection, setting up a printer, and creating a network of PCs.

A wizard will present a series of screens, each asking you to select options or to type in information.

You don't have to go looking for the right wizard to accomplish a task. Windows XP presents the correct wizard the first time you set up a new function or piece of hardware.

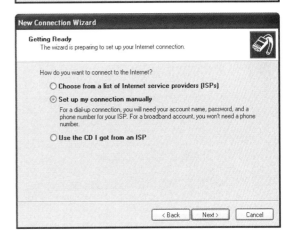

# get dialog box help

Windows XP offers several different ways to get answers to your questions about what the commands in dialog boxes do. Of course, you can search the main help system by going to the Start menu and selecting Help and Support. This is the hard way, as it requires you to search the Help system

There is a better way to find out specifically what an option or button in a dialog box does.

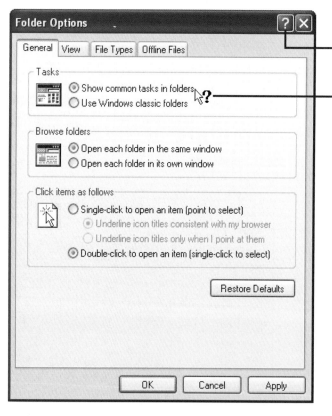

**1** Click the question mark at the top-right of a dialog box.

**2** A question mark appears next to the cursor arrow. Move the cursor/question mark over a command or button that you want to know about and click.

**explore windows xp customization**

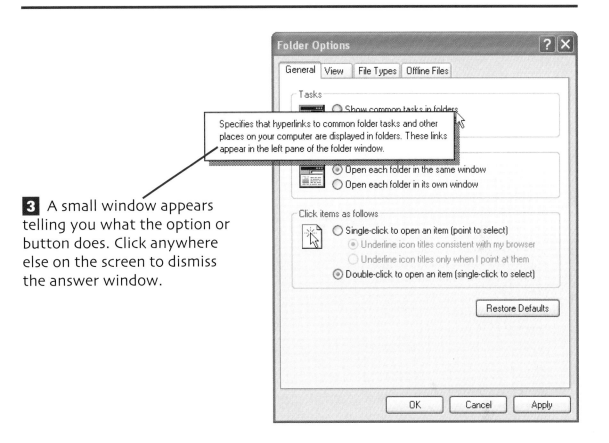

**3** A small window appears telling you what the option or button does. Click anywhere else on the screen to dismiss the answer window.

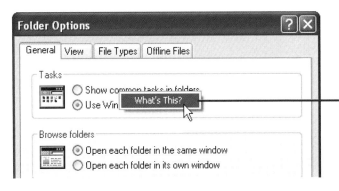

Another way to bring up the same pop-up window is to right-click a command or button in the dialog box. This brings up a small shortcut menu with a single item in it: What's This?. Click on What's This? and the answer appears.

# extra bits

## properties windows p. 3

- In any dialog box, the OK button enacts the changes you just made to the settings and closes the dialog box.
- The Apply button also makes the change, but keeps the dialog box open.

## use the control panel p. 4

- When the Control Panel is in classic view, you can rearrange and change the size of icons just as you can documents in a folder window. Just go to the View menu and select an option.

## get dialog box help p. 6

- Sometimes the help you get in a dialog box is so specific that you can't tell what it means. If you can't find what you're looking for in the Help and Support Center in the Start menu, you can look online. Click the Support icon at the top of the Help and Support Center window. Your Web browser will launch and take you to Microsoft's support Web site.

**explore windows xp customization**

# 2. personalize the desktop

The Desktop is what's on your monitor when you've opened Windows but don't have any programs open. In this chapter you'll learn how to change Microsoft's default Desktop to make it your own.

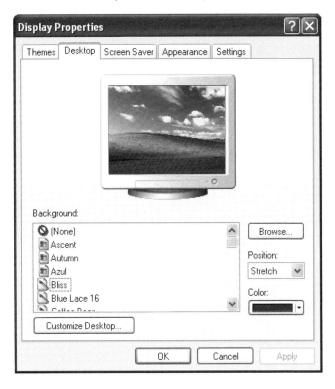

Working with the Display Properties dialog box, you can replace the standard Desktop picture with a favorite family photo, a solid color, or an abstract pattern. In the Display Properties dialog box you can also make the Desktop icons bigger or smaller, or change the size of everything on your computer screen.

# replace desktop photo

Sick of the grassy hill? Have a nice picture you'd rather look at? You can replace the standard desktop picture with your own digital photo (such as a JPEG file) from your hard disk. Use a horizontally oriented photo to have it automatically fit to the Desktop.

**1** Right-click on the desktop and select Properties from the shortcut list.

**2** Click the Desktop tab.

**3** Click the Browse button to bring up the Browser window.

If you don't have your own photo, Windows XP has many pictures and patterns to choose from in the Background field. You'll find the grassy hill listed here, going by the name of Bliss.

**personalize the desktop**

**4** Navigate through your folders to find the picture you'd like to use.

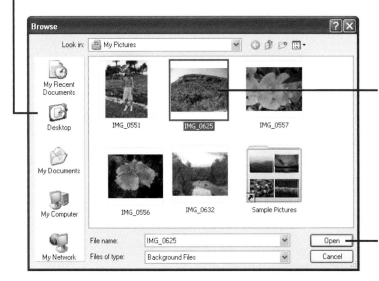

**5** When you find your photo, click on it to select it.

**6** Click the Open button. The Browse window will close, bringing you back to the Properties window.

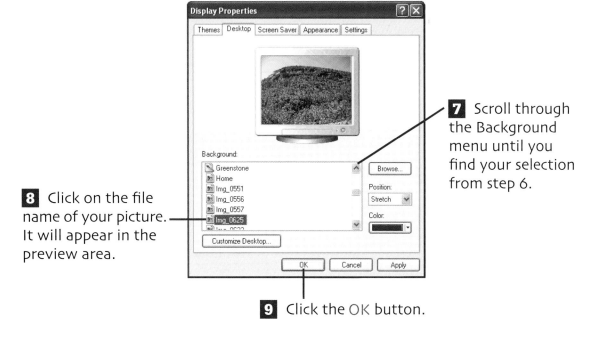

**7** Scroll through the Background menu until you find your selection from step 6.

**8** Click on the file name of your picture. It will appear in the preview area.

**9** Click the OK button.

# replace desktop photo

After the Display Properties window closes, you'll see your photo where the standard desktop picture used to be.

Windows will shrink or stretch your photo to fit the screen if your image doesn't fit exactly. If your picture is too small you can tell Windows to simply center the picture at full size.

**personalize the desktop**

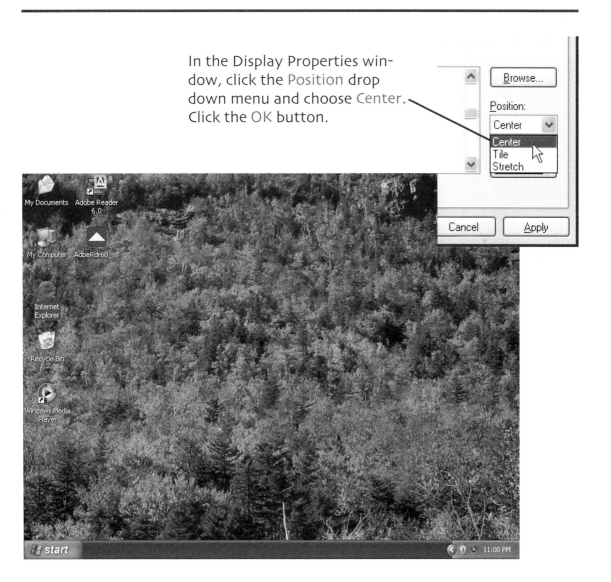

In the Display Properties window, click the Position drop down menu and choose Center. Click the OK button.

Position:

Center

Center
Tile
Stretch

Browse...

Cancel          Apply

You can see that the desktop picture here is larger than on the facing page, with the outside edges cut off. In this case, it's a pleasing effect, but might not be with other photos.

# change desktop size

If your Desktop is getting crowded with icons that you don't want to remove, making them smaller will help make your Desktop appear less cluttered and create more space. We can do this by adjusting the the display resolution.

For instance, this screen, set at 640x480 pixels, barely has enough room for the Start menu.

**personalize the desktop**

When you increase the resolution (to 1152x768 pixels), everything shrinks, giving you more room on the Desktop for icons, windows, and other objects.

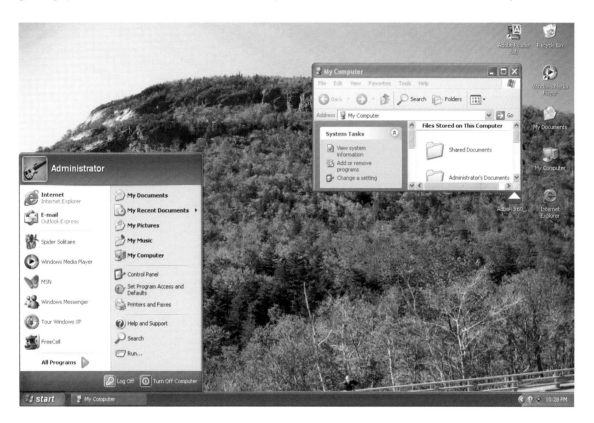

**1** Right-click on the Desktop and select Properties from the shortcut menu.

# change desktop size (cont.)

**2** Click the Settings tab.

**3** Drag the Screen resolution slider bar to change the pixel resolution.

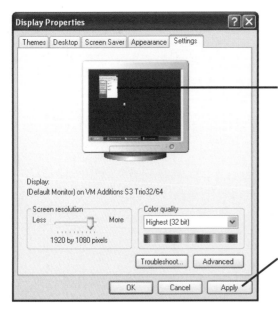

**4** Watch the sample area as you move the slider back and forth. You'll see the sample window and Desktop icon shrink as you increase the screen resolution, and grow as you decrease the resolution.

**5** Click the Apply button to see what your selection will look like on your full Desktop.

　　　　　　　　　　**personalize the desktop**

**6** Your Desktop resolution changes, but only temporarily. The Monitor Settings dialog box appears telling you that it will revert to the previous setting in a few seconds. If you do nothing, your Desktop will revert to the previous resolution when the count down reaches zero seconds. By clicking the No button you'll cancel the change without waiting for the countdown.

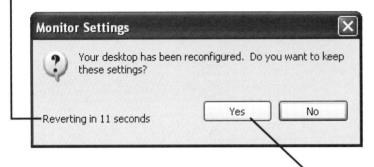

**7** To accept the new resolution, click Yes before the countdown ends.

**8** Click OK to close the Display Properties dialog box.

# switch themes

Switching themes is the easiest way to change the way Windows XP looks. In the Themes tab, you can change the look of windows, menus, and buttons, and select new fonts and colors. If you prefer the way previous versions of Windows looked, no problem. Just switch to the Classic theme.

**1** Right-click on the Desktop and select Properties from the shortcut list.

**2** In the Display Properties dialog box, click the Themes tab.

**3** From the Theme drop-down menu, select Windows Classic.

The Sample area displays the look of the current theme. Here, the Windows XP theme is displayed. The window called Active Window isn't a real window; It's just a sample of what a window looks like in the current theme.

**personalize the desktop**

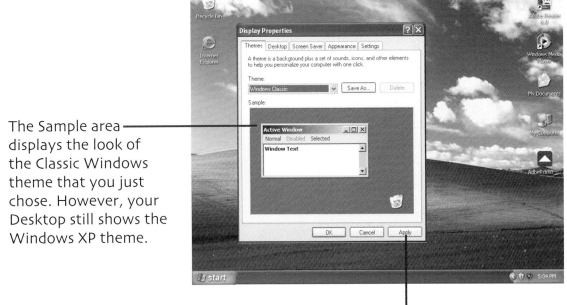

The Sample area displays the look of the Classic Windows theme that you just chose. However, your Desktop still shows the Windows XP theme.

**4** To set Windows to the new theme, click the Apply button.

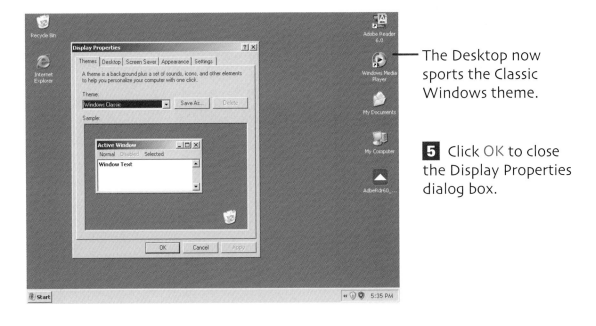

The Desktop now sports the Classic Windows theme.

**5** Click OK to close the Display Properties dialog box.

**personalize the desktop**

# enlarge desktop items

You don't have to be satisfied with the themes provided. Within a theme, you can change the look and feel of icons, the size and types of fonts, and the way windows and buttons look. You can also change the color scheme of a theme. Here, we're going to change the look of the Desktop icons.

**1** Right-click on the Desktop and select Properties from the shortcut list.

**2** In the Display Properties dialog box, click the Appearance tab.

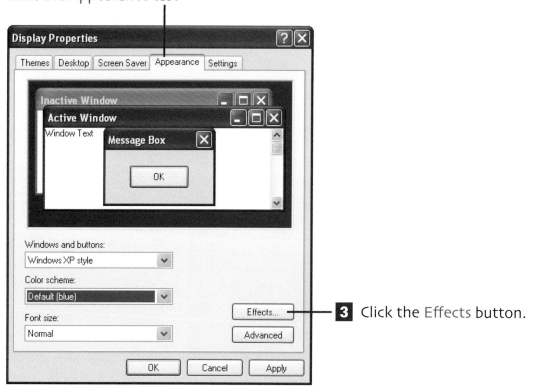

**3** Click the Effects button.

**personalize the desktop**

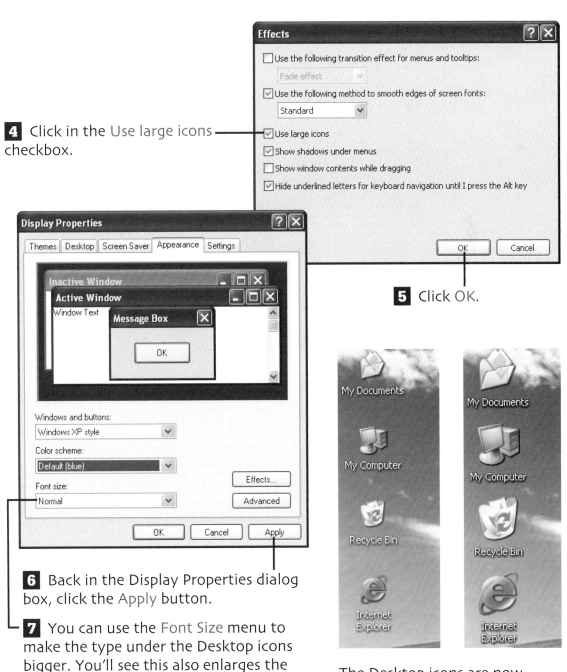

**Effects**

☐ Use the following transition effect for menus and tooltips:

Fade effect ▾

☑ Use the following method to smooth edges of screen fonts:

Standard ▾

☑ Use large icons

☑ Show shadows under menus

☐ Show window contents while dragging

☑ Hide underlined letters for keyboard navigation until I press the Alt key

OK    Cancel

**4** Click in the Use large icons checkbox.

**5** Click OK.

**Display Properties**

Themes | Desktop | Screen Saver | Appearance | Settings

Inactive Window

Active Window

Window Text

Message Box

OK

Windows and buttons:

Windows XP style ▾

Color scheme:

Default (blue) ▾

Font size:

Normal ▾

Effects...

Advanced

OK    Cancel    Apply

My Documents

My Computer

Recycle Bin

Internet Explorer

My Documents

My Computer

Recycle Bin

Internet Explorer

**6** Back in the Display Properties dialog box, click the Apply button.

**7** You can use the Font Size menu to make the type under the Desktop icons bigger. You'll see this also enlarges the text in title bars and in the Start menu.

The Desktop icons are now enlarged, as shown on the right.

**personalize the desktop**

# extra bits

## replace desktop photo p. 10

- If you don't know the pixel resolution of a photo, it's easy to find out. Right-click it and choose Properties from the shortcut menu. Next, click the Summary tab, then the Advanced button. The dialog box will show the height and width of the photo in pixels.

- You don't need to switch to the Windows Classic theme in order to set the Desktop to a solid color. Right-click the Desktop and select Properties. Click the Desktop tab. Under background, select None. Now choose a color from the Color menu. Click the Apply button to see your color on the Desktop.

## switch themes p. 18

- I have to admit, switching between Windows XP and Classic Windows themes isn't the most exciting way to customize your desktop. However, you can add more themes that will give you a variety of new looks for Windows.

There are many sites you can visit to buy themes and even download free themes. PC World magazine has a good selection of free themes at http://www.pcworld. com/downloads/.

Microsoft will sell you new themes as part of its $30 Microsoft Plus Pack. To get to Microsoft's Web page, right click your desktop to open the Display Properties dialog box, click the Themes tab, and select More Themes online.

# 3. customize toolbars and taskbar

The Taskbar is a jumping off point for opening folders and files. It includes the Start button and a few icons that open programs. You can add more icons to have one-click access to the programs you need. There are also toolbars hidden away in the Taskbar that give you access to even more of your files and folders.

Microsoft stretches the meaning of toolbar beyond that of a horizontal strip with icons on it. Windows XP toolbars can also exist as vertical strips or even as menus on the Taskbar or floating windows.

# add new toolbar

Desktop toolbars can take several forms. In addition to the traditional icon-studded horizontal, Desktop toolbars can appear as items on the Taskbar, and as stand-alone windows. You can add one or more of the toolbars that come with Windows XP. You can also create your own customized toolbar containing the contents of one of your folders.

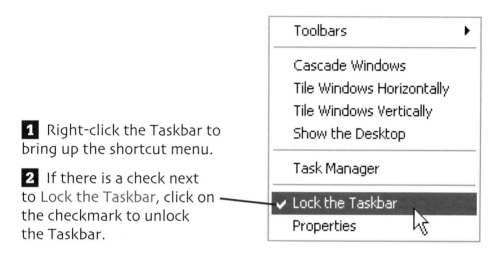

**1** Right-click the Taskbar to bring up the shortcut menu.

**2** If there is a check next to Lock the Taskbar, click on the checkmark to unlock the Taskbar.

This is a locked Taskbar.

This is an unlocked Taskbar, which sports these double dotted lines. An unlocked Taskbar is also a little taller.

**customize toolbars and taskbar**

**3** In the shortcut menu that you just opened, move the cursor to Toolbars at the top of the menu.

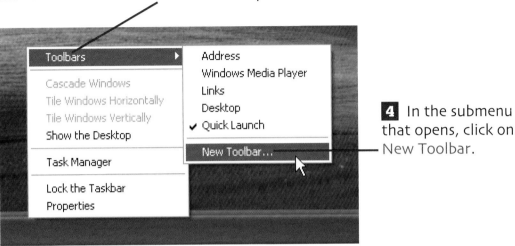

**4** In the submenu that opens, click on New Toolbar.

**5** In the New Toolbar dialog box, navigate to the folder that you would like to put in the toolbar. Here, we are choosing the folder called Project Files.

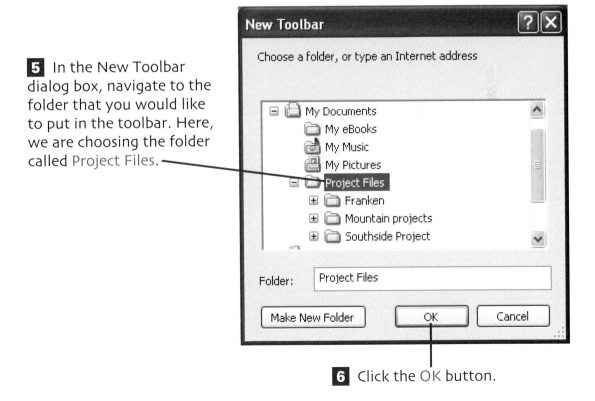

**6** Click the OK button.

**customize toolbars and taskbar**

# add new toolbar (cont.)

**7** A toolbar will appear in the Taskbar with the name of the folder you choose, which is Project Files in this example. Click the double arrows to open the toolbar's menu.

**8** You can now navigate through the hierarchical menus to the folder or file you'd like to open.

**customize toolbars and taskbar**

# rearrange the toolbar

Once you activate a toolbar, you can move it off of the Taskbar to anywhere on the Desktop.

**1** Drag your toolbar from the Taskbar and drop it onto the Desktop. Your toolbar transforms into a window known as a floating toolbar. ————————————

**2** Drag the floating toolbar to the top or sides of the screen. The window transforms into a fixed toolbar. This fixed toolbar is on the right side of the screen. ————

If you change your mind, you can change the fixed toolbar back into a floating toolbar by dragging from these dotted lines.

# rearrange the toolbar

**3** The folder icons are a bit small, but you can enlarge them. Right-click on a blank spot on the toolbar (not on one of the icons). Click View and then Large Icons.

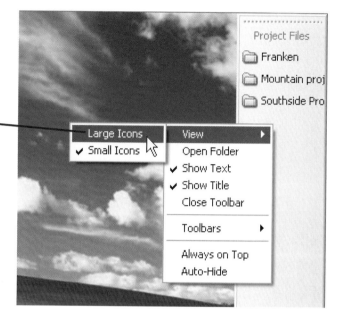

The toolbar's icons are now bigger. Each icon is a button; click and it will open the folder or file depicted.

**customize toolbars and taskbar**

**4** You can add file and folder shortcuts by dragging them to the toolbar. You can even drag the My Computer icon here to make a shortcut.

The files that you drag to the toolbar will have filenames that begin with "Shortcut to," which isn't very helpful.

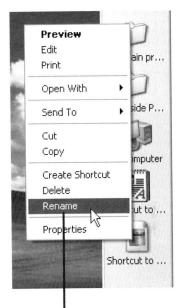

**5** You can change the name of the shortcut by right-clicking the icon and selecting Rename.

**6** Delete Shortcut to from the file name.

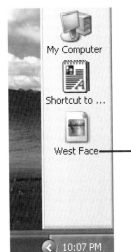

| Rename | |
|---|---|
| New name: | Shortcut to West Face |

OK    Cancel

The shortcut in the toolbar now has a name that you can recognize.

# add taskbar icons

In addition to the Start menu and minimized windows, the Taskbar holds icons that let you quickly open programs. You can add programs to the Taskbar for easy access.

The Quick Launch toolbar, the area next to the Start menu on the left side of the Taskbar, contains icons for certain programs. Click one, and the program opens. You can easily add another program by dragging it to the Quick Launch toolbar. In this example, we'll add Outlook Express.

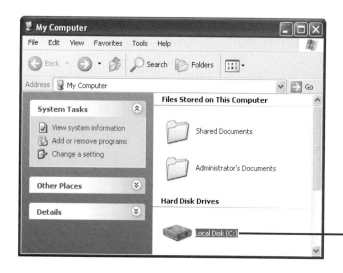

**1** To find your program, open My Computer and double-click Local Disk.

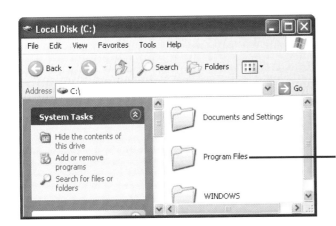

**2** Double-click Program Files.

**3** Scroll through the list of programs, find the folder with your program, and open it.

**4** Drag the program file to the middle of the Quick Launch toolbar on the Taskbar.

**customize toolbars and taskbar**

# add taskbar icons (cont.)

The program's icon is now on the Taskbar. You can click it to open your program whenever you need it.

Notice that the Windows Media Player icon has been pushed off of the Taskbar. You'll find it in the pop-up menu if you click the double arrow.

Fortunately, you can get the Windows Media Player icon back on the Taskbar by widening the Quick Launch area.

**5** Right-click an empty space on the Taskbar and select Lock the Taskbar to remove the checkmark. The Taskbar is now unlocked.

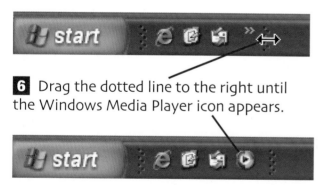

**6** Drag the dotted line to the right until the Windows Media Player icon appears.

**customize toolbars and taskbar**

# add player to taskbar

Ordinarily, when you click the Taskbar's Windows Media Player icon, the Player's window appears. You can add a smaller version of the Media Player right in the Taskbar that will be available to you while other programs are open.

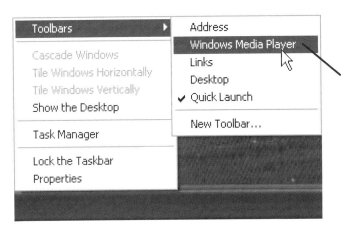

**1** Right-click an empty area of the Windows toolbar. Click Toolbars and choose Windows Media Player.

**2** Click the Windows Media Player icon in the Taskbar. The player opens.

**3** Minimize the Media Player window.

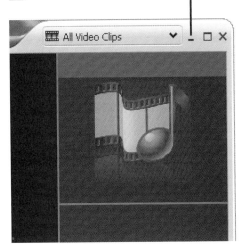

Instead of the standard window, the minimized window is a tiny but fully functional Media Player, which you can use to play movies and music.

# extra bits

## add new toolbars p. 24

- You can remove a toolbar from the Taskbar or from the side of the screen by dragging it to the middle of the Desktop.

  The toolbar turns into a floating toolbar window. To dismiss it, just click the X button in its upper right corner.

## add taskbar icons p. 30

- The Taskbar doesn't have to sit on the bottom of the screen. You can move to the top or sides of your screen simply by unlocking it and dragging it.

  When you move the Taskbar, everything on it goes with it, including the Start menu and any items you've installed.

# 4. customize the start menu

The Start menu is the chief method of getting to your programs and files. There are a number of ways to customize the Start menu to better suit your needs.

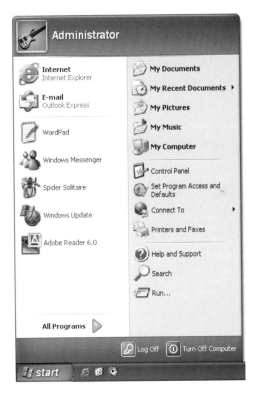

The left side of the Start menu contains icons representing programs. The top left icons are always present. The bottom left area lists programs you've recently used. In this chapter, you'll change the way these icons look and act.

The right side of the Start menu gives you access to your files, settings, the Help system, and other features of Windows XP. In this chapter, you'll convert some of these icons into menus. You'll also remove and add items to the Start menu.

# restyle the start menu

There are lots of ways you can change the look of the Start menu. Here, we're going to shrink the size of the left-side icons and allow Windows to display more of them.

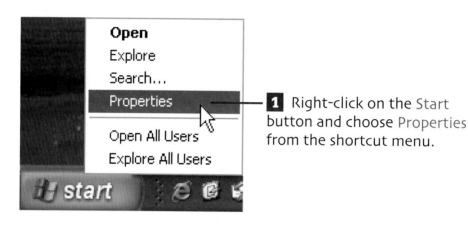

**1** Right-click on the Start button and choose Properties from the shortcut menu.

**2** Click the Customize button in the Properties dialog box.

**customize the start menu**

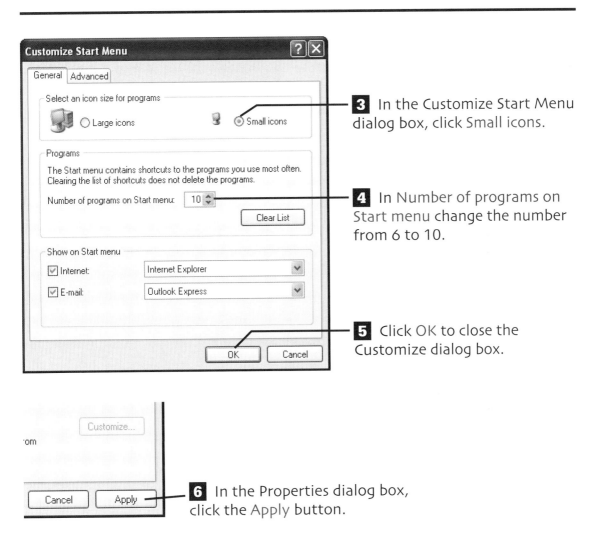

**3** In the Customize Start Menu dialog box, click Small icons.

**4** In Number of programs on Start menu change the number from 6 to 10.

**5** Click OK to close the Customize dialog box.

**6** In the Properties dialog box, click the Apply button.

# restyle the start menu

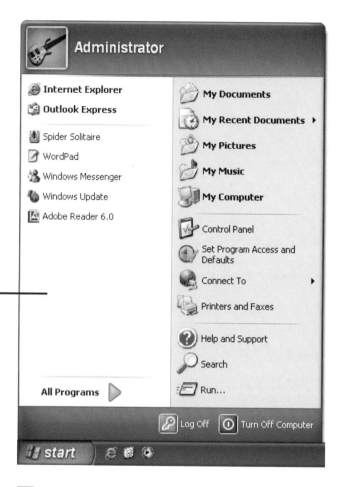

**7** Go back to the start menu to see the result of your changes. You'll see that there is now space on the left side of the Start menu to hold more program icons.

**8** If you are satisfied with the result, click OK in the Properties dialog box to close the dialog.

**customize the start menu**

# convert links to menus

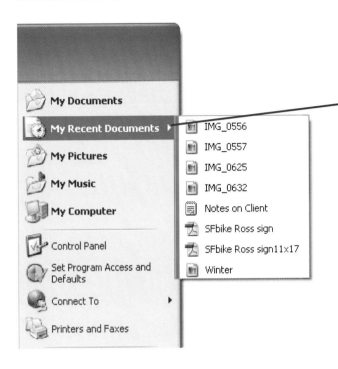

Most of the icons on the right side of the Start menu open a new window when you click on them. Items that have an arrow next them are hierarchical menus that let you delve into the contents.

Next, we're going to change the My Document and My Computer links into hierarchical menus.

**1** Right-click on the Start button and choose Properties from the shortcut menu.

**2** Click the Customize button in the Properties dialog box.

**3** In the Customize dialog, click the Advanced tab.

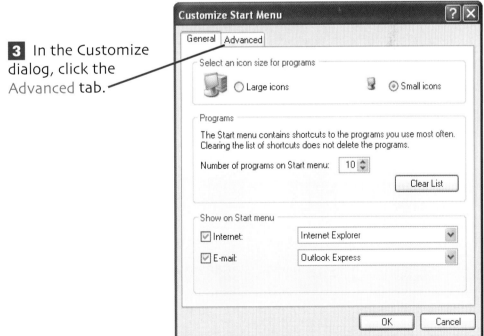

# convert links to menus

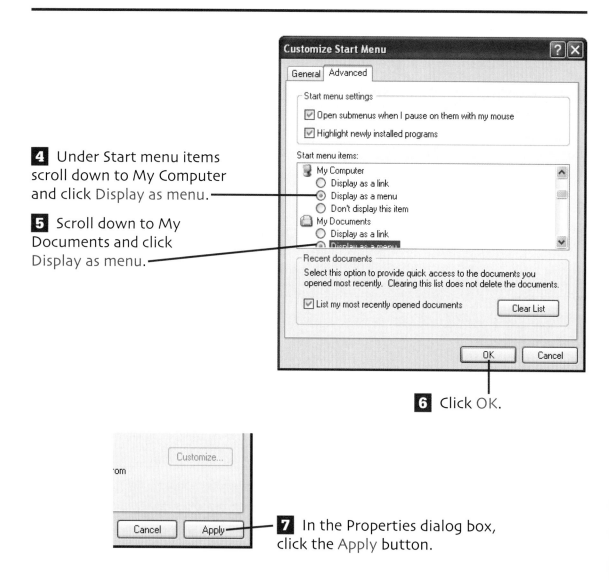

**4** Under Start menu items scroll down to My Computer and click Display as menu.

**5** Scroll down to My Documents and click Display as menu.

Customize Start Menu

General | Advanced

Start menu settings
☑ Open submenus when I pause on them with my mouse
☑ Highlight newly installed programs

Start menu items:
- My Computer
  - ○ Display as a link
  - ⦿ Display as a menu
  - ○ Don't display this item
- My Documents
  - ○ Display as a link
  - ⦿ Display as a menu

Recent documents
Select this option to provide quick access to the documents you opened most recently. Clearing this list does not delete the documents.

☑ List my most recently opened documents    [ Clear List ]

[ OK ]  [ Cancel ]

**6** Click OK.

Customize...
om
[ Cancel ]  [ Apply ]

**7** In the Properties dialog box, click the Apply button.

**customize the start menu**

**8** Go back to the Start menu to see the result of your changes. You can now click on My Computer and My Documents to select an item several levels down.

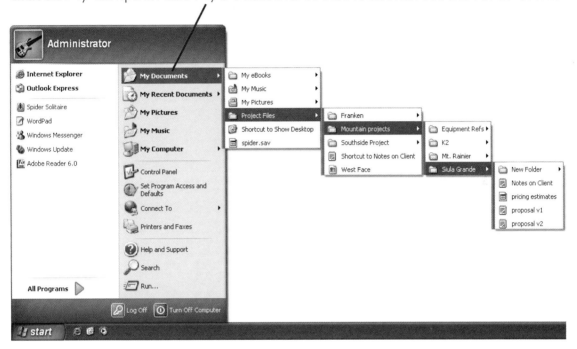

**9** If you are satisfied with the result, click OK in the Properties dialog box to close the dialog.

# add a program

The left side of the Start menu is handy for opening programs with a single click. The icons on the upper left are always there for your use, while the icons below are programs you recently opened. For other programs, you have to dig through the Programs submenu.

Here you'll add a program to the top left of the menu. Windows calls this "pinning" a program to the Start menu. There are two ways to do this.

If the program is already in the recently opened portion of the Start menu, simply drag it up to the top left area of the Start menu.

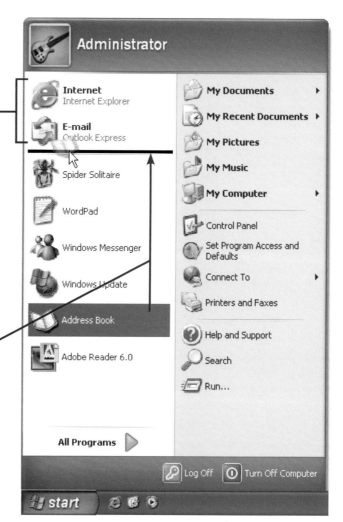

If the program is not in the Start menu, you can use the All Programs menu.

**1** Open the Start menu, click All Programs, and navigate through the hierarchical menus to your program.

**2** Right-click your program.

**3** In the shortcut menu, select Pin to Start menu.

With either method, the result is the same: your program is pinned to the top of the Start menu.

**customize the start menu**

# add a folder

Programs aren't the only items you can pin to the left side of the Start menu. You can place a shortcut to a folder on the Start menu.

You can drag a folder from the Desktop, from a window, or from a hierarchical menu in the Start menu. Here, you're going to drag your folder from Windows Explorer.

**1** Right-click the Start menu and choose Explore from shortcut menu.

**2** Windows Explorer will open. Locate your folder and drag it onto the Start menu button.

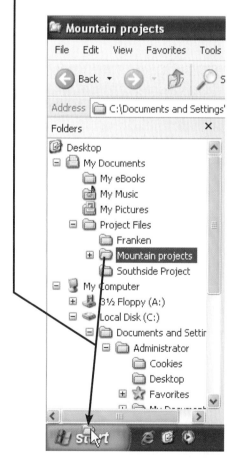

The Start menu now includes your folder at the top left. If you click the folder icon its window will open.

**customize the start menu**

# delete a menu item

Of course, nothing is forever, including decisions you make in Windows XP. If you no longer need an item that is pinned to the top left of the Start menu, you can remove it.

Right-click the item in the Start menu and select Remove from This List. The item will disappear from the Start menu, but the original folder or program is still in your PC.

When you right-click on a program at the top left of the Start menu, you get an additional choice, Unpin from Start menu. When you select this, the program icon will move to the list of recent programs below the line.

# extra bits

**restyle the start menu** p. 36

- You may have noticed that the Start menu's Properties dialog box gives you a Classic Windows Start menu option.

  This option doesn't just serve as nostalgia for Windows past. It offers a more stream-lined Start menu, one that takes less screen space.

  The classic Start menu has its own customization dialog box with customization features that are different from those of the standard Start menu.

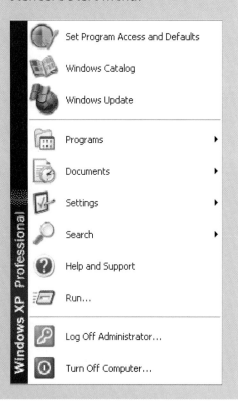

**convert links to menus** p. 40

- You may have noticed throughout this chapter that the Start menu has a submenu called My Recent Documents. In Windows XP Professional, this is always turned on. In Windows XP Home Edition, you'll have to turn on My Recent Documents to see it in the Start menu. Just right-click Start and click Properties. Then click Customize and select List my most recently opened documents. (Windows XP Professional doesn't give you the option to turn off My Recent Documents.)

**add a folder** p. 44

- Another way to bring up Windows Explorer is to press Windows-E.

# 5. rearrange desktop items

The previous chapters have been focused in and around the Desktop—how to personalize the Desktop, the Taskbar, and the Start menu. In this chapter, you'll learn how to place different types of items on the Desktop, and how to remove others.

The Desktop is another place to put files and folders for easy access. Windows XP gives you special techniques for adding different types of items to the Desktop. You'll also learn how to put Desktop items in the Taskbar.

With this ability to add items, the Desktop can easily become cluttered. You'll learn how to clean up the Desktop with the tools of Windows XP.

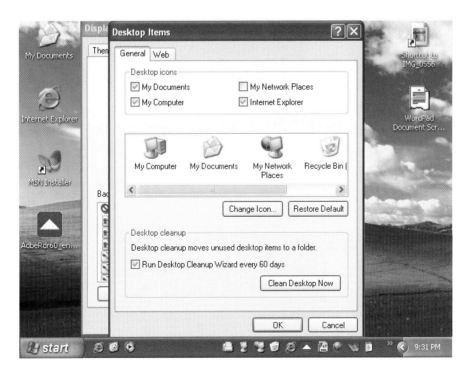

# place files and folders

You know from previous versions of Windows that you can drag and drop folders from a window to the Desktop. Windows XP offers several other ways of bringing your work out onto the Desktop.

First, let's look at another kind of drag-and-drop called a right drag.

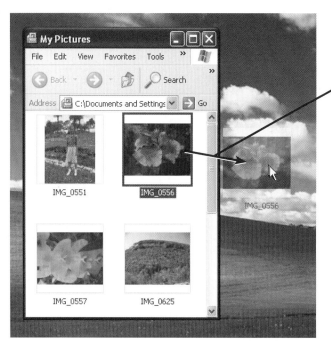

**1** Open a folder containing a file or folder that you want to place on the Desktop.

**2** Click on the file with the right mouse button and drag it to the Desktop. As long as you hold the right mouse button down, it looks like an ordinary drag-and-drop.

**rearrange desktop items**

**3** Release the right mouse button. Instead of the usual file icon on the Desktop, you'll see a shortcut menu.

**4** Select one of the options.

Move Here is just like an ordinary drag-and-drop; the file moves out of the folder onto the Desktop.

Copy Here creates a new file on the Desktop while keeping your original file in its place.

Create Shortcuts Here is the best of both worlds: it keeps your original file in its original location, but creates a small pointer file, the shortcut, that takes up a fraction of the hard drive's space that a copy of a big graphic file might take.

Shortcuts have the same icon as the original file except for an arrow in the lower-left corner.

You don't need the words Shortcut to in the file name. You can change the name of the original file or of the shortcut. Double-clicking the shortcut will open the original file or folder.

**rearrange desktop items**                                          **49**

# hide standard icons

There are serveral places you can access My Computer, Internet Explorer, and My Documents, so you may not need them cluttering up the Desktop. You can choose to hide some or all of these standard Desktop icons.

**1** Right-click on a blank spot on the Desktop and choose Properties from the pop-up menu.

**2** In the Display properties dialog box, click the Desktop tab.

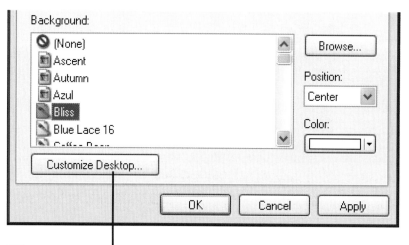

**3** Click the Customize Desktop button.

**rearrange desktop items**

**4** In the Desktop Items dialog box you'll find four standard Windows Desktop icons listed. If you want to hide the icon, make sure there is no checkmark next to it. If you want the icon to appear on the Desktop, make sure there is a checkmark next to it.

**5** Click OK to close the Desktop Items dialog box.

**6** Click OK to close the Display Properties dialog box.

If you removed all the check-marks in Step 4, the four standard Windows icons will now be gone from the Desktop.

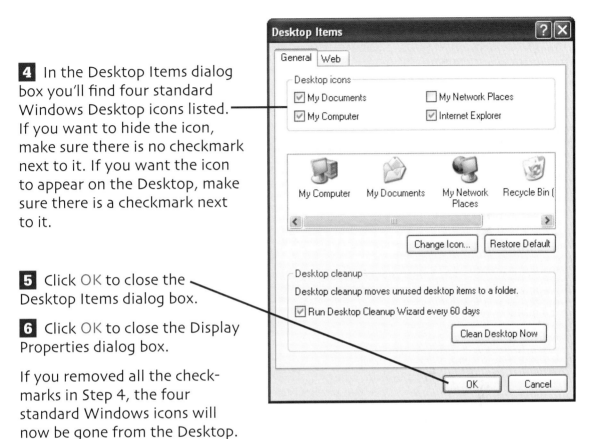

**Desktop Items** [?][X]

General | Web

Desktop icons
☑ My Documents ☐ My Network Places
☑ My Computer ☑ Internet Explorer

My Computer   My Documents   My Network   Recycle Bin (
Places

◄ ◄                    ►

[ Change Icon... ]  [ Restore Default ]

Desktop cleanup
Desktop cleanup moves unused desktop items to a folder.
☑ Run Desktop Cleanup Wizard every 60 days

[ Clean Desktop Now ]

[ OK ]  [ Cancel ]

# cleanup the desktop

Your new PC probably came with demostration software that included annoying Desktop shortcut icons. In addition, programs that you install often create shortcuts you don't need.

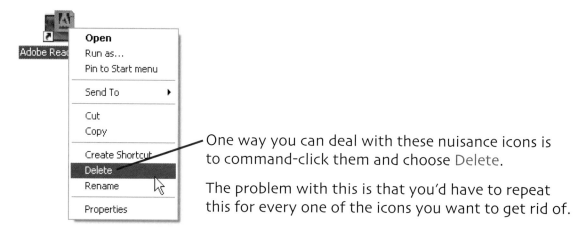

One way you can deal with these nuisance icons is to command-click them and choose Delete.

The problem with this is that you'd have to repeat this for every one of the icons you want to get rid of.

A better method is to have Windows move icons that you haven't been using recently off of your Desktop and into a folder called Unused Desktop Shortcuts.

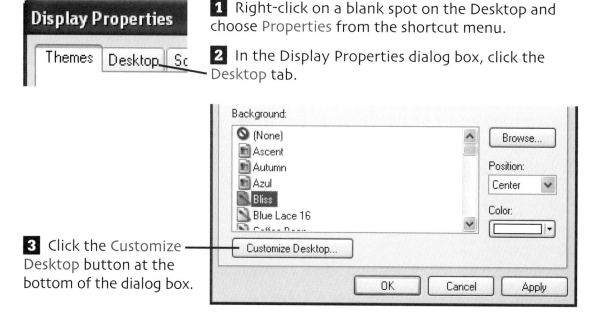

**1** Right-click on a blank spot on the Desktop and choose Properties from the shortcut menu.

**2** In the Display Properties dialog box, click the Desktop tab.

**3** Click the Customize Desktop button at the bottom of the dialog box.

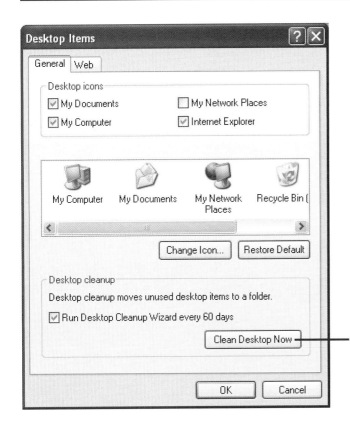

**4** In the Desktop Items dialog box, click the Clean Desktop Now button.

**5** The Desktop Cleanup Wizard will appear. Click the Next button.

**rearrange desktop items**

# cleanup the desktop (cont.)

**6** The Wizard will now list the shortcuts on your Desktop. Those that you haven't used recently will have a checkmark next to them. These will be moved off of the Desktop. Shortcuts that you have used recently will not have a check-mark and will be left on the Desktop. If you want to make any changes, you can check and uncheck any item in the list.

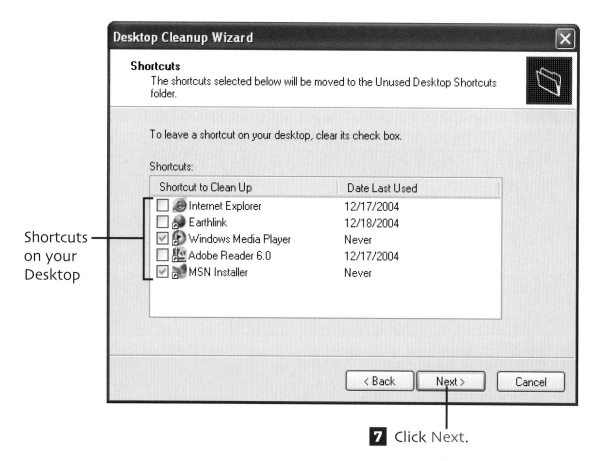

Shortcuts on your Desktop

**7** Click Next.

**8** A final screen will appear listing the shortcut files you want to remove. If this is correct, click Finish. If not, click Back.

You'll notice back in step 4 that there was an option called Desktop Cleanup Wizard every 60 days. If you aren't adding a lot of new shortcuts, it might be worthwhile to uncheck it.

**rearrange desktop items**

# add icons to taskbar

Having items on the Desktop can be very handy—unless you have a bunch of windows open. Instead, you can add a Desktop toolbar to the Taskbar to give you access to Desktop icons, whether they represent programs, documents, or folders.

**1** Right-click an empty space on the Taskbar and choose Toolbars, then Desktop, from the shortcut menu.

**2** Click the double-arrows next to the word Desktop that has appeared on the right side of the Toolbar. A menu pops up listing your desktop icons.

**3** You can now put these Desktop icons right on the Taskbar. Right-click the word Desktop (not the double arrows) and select Lock the Taskbar to remove the check next to it. The Taskbar is now unlocked.

# add icons to taskbar (cont.)

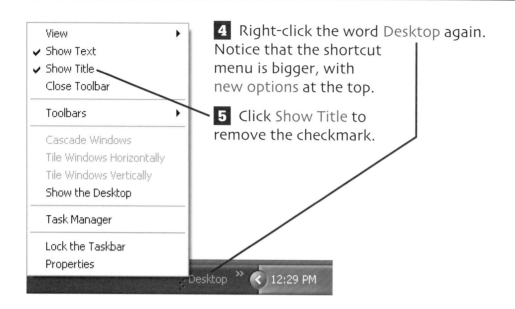

| |
|---|
| View ▶ |
| ✓ Show Text |
| ✓ Show Title |
| Close Toolbar |
| |
| Toolbars ▶ |
| |
| Cascade Windows |
| Tile Windows Horizontally |
| Tile Windows Vertically |
| Show the Desktop |
| |
| Task Manager |
| |
| Lock the Taskbar |
| Properties |

**4** Right-click the word Desktop again. Notice that the shortcut menu is bigger, with new options at the top.

**5** Click Show Title to remove the checkmark.

Desktop » ◀ 12:29 PM

Internet Explorer
Earthlink
Windows Media Player
Adobe Reader 6.0
New Text Document
MSN Installer
AdbeRdr60_enu_full

🗐 My Documents   🖳 My Computer   🖳 My Network Places   🗑 Recycle Bin   » ◀ 1:18 PM

The word Desktop has disappeared. Your Taskbar will now hold as many of your items that fit.

The rest are displayed in the double-arrow menu.

**rearrange desktop items**

**6** If you want all of your Desktop icons to fit on the Taskbar, you'll have to get rid of the text next to the icons. Right-click on the area on the Taskbar where the word Desktop used to be and click Show Text to remove the checkmark.

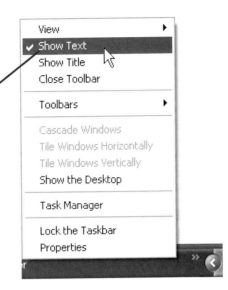

Now all of your Desktop icons can fit on the Taskbar (unless you really have a lot of Desktop items).

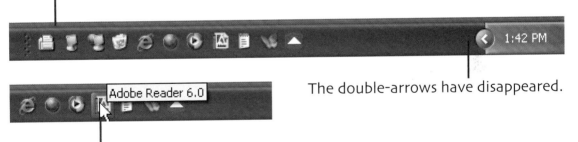

The double-arrows have disappeared.

Hold the cursor arrow over an icon, a description of the item will appear.

**rearrange desktop items**

# extra bits

## place files and folders p. 48

- Did you know that the documents and shortcut files on the Desktop actually sit inside a folder called, well, Desktop?

  It's in the Documents and Settings folder, inside a folder named after your user name.

  Add an item to the Desktop folder and it appears on the Desktop.

- Have you ever wanted easy access to a small portion of a file? You don't have to create a new document—just create a scrap.

  To create a scrap, simply select some text—a paragraph, sentence, or phrase—and drag it from the document window to the Desktop. A new file is created that has an icon with a jagged bottom.

WordPad
Document Scrap
'winter of our...'

## cleanup the desktop p. 52

- Another way to quickly access your Desktop icons is with a key command. You can press Windows-D to minimize all of the open windows at the same time.

  This technique will even minimize windows that don't have a minimize button, such as dialog boxes and the Control Panel.

  Pressing Windows-D again will restore all of the windows you just minimized—unless you've opened, minimized, or restored any windows since hitting the command. If that's the case, Windows-D will only work on the last window you worked with.

# 6. customize folders and windows

Windows XP offers plenty of options for customizing the look and function of your windows and folders in order to better fit the way you work. You can remove interface elements that you don't use, change the way icons look and work, and display information about files in a folder window. Here are some examples of the changes you can make:

You can add pictures to folder icons.

You can hide or modify Window toolbars.

You can hide the pane on the left side of the window and bring it back when you need it.

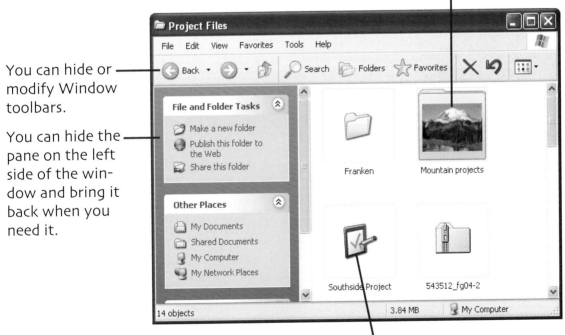

You can view the file and folder icons in different sizes and sort them in different ways.

You can also replace a folder icon with something new.

In this chapter, you'll be making all of these changes. We'll begin with changing the look of the windows. Then we'll change the look of the folder contents.

# hide the left pane

The links pane on the left side of the folder windows provides links to related places and tasks. But you might not always need it. You might want to use the space to show files instead. To do this, you can temporarily turn off the left pane.

**1** Go to the Tools menu of the folder you want to change and select Folder Options.

**2** On the General Tab, under Tasks, click Use Windows classic folders.

The links pane on the left has now disappeared from all folders.

**customize folders and windows**

# create a shortcut

You may not want the side pane hidden all of the time; you may need it for viewing some folders and not for others. While you can't specify this setting for different folders, you can make it easy to open the Folder Options dialog. You'll create a shortcut.

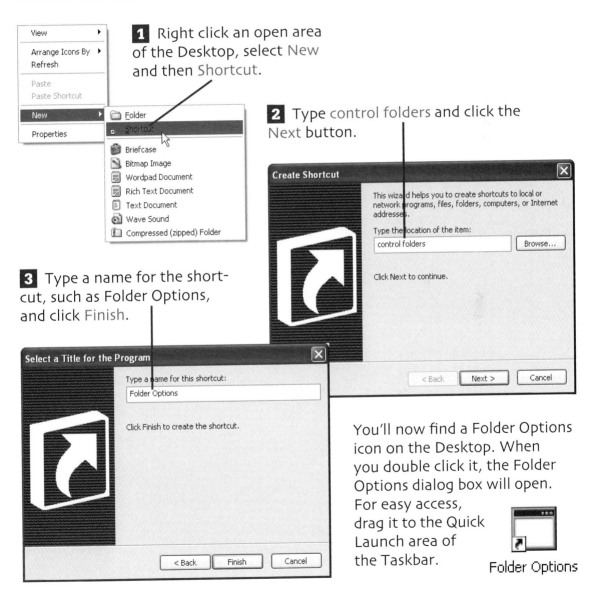

**1** Right click an open area of the Desktop, select New and then Shortcut.

**2** Type control folders and click the Next button.

**3** Type a name for the shortcut, such as Folder Options, and click Finish.

You'll now find a Folder Options icon on the Desktop. When you double click it, the Folder Options dialog box will open. For easy access, drag it to the Quick Launch area of the Taskbar.

Folder Options

# modify folder toolbars

Folder windows have several toolbars that you can hide or modify. Each toolbar has a different set of functions that can often be found in the related menus, making the toolbar unnecessary.

The Address toolbar. You use the Address bar to type the path of a folder to go directly to that folder or to the Internet. If you don't type folder paths, you can hide the Address bar without missing much.

The Buttons toolbar. Similar to a Web browser toolbar, the Buttons toolbar lets you navigate between folders on your PC. The Buttons toolbar is completely customizable.

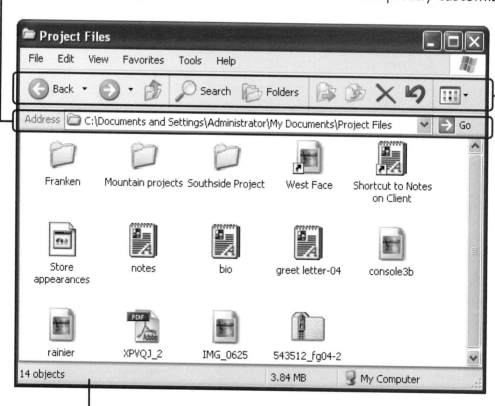

The Status bar. This gives you information on the open folder, or of a selected file or folder, in the open folder window.

First, we'll hide the Address bar.

Go to the View menu, move the mouse to Toolbars, and click Address bar. The Address bar will disapear.

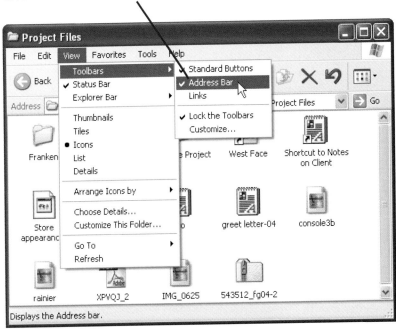

We're now going to modify the icon toolbar, remove some icons, add some new ones, and move things around a bit.

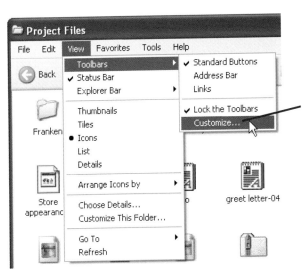

**1** In the View menu, move the mouse to Toolbars and then click Customize.

**customize folders and windows**

# modify folder toolbars

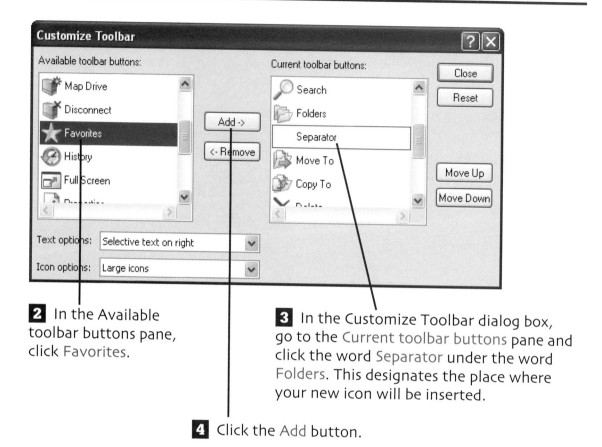

**2** In the Available toolbar buttons pane, click Favorites.

**3** In the Customize Toolbar dialog box, go to the Current toolbar buttons pane and click the word Separator under the word Folders. This designates the place where your new icon will be inserted.

**4** Click the Add button.

**customize folders and windows**

The Favorites icon has been added above the separator.

**5** Now click Move To below it and click Remove. Do the same for Copy to.

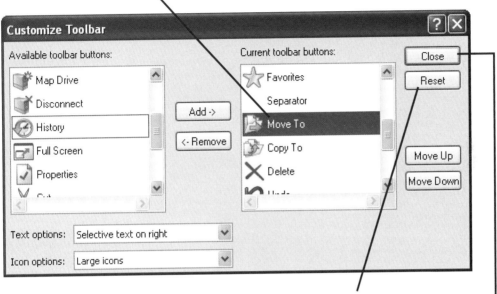

**6** You can rearrange the icons and separators on the toolbar by dragging them up and down in the Current toolbar buttons pane. Items at the top of the list will be located on the left of the toolbar; bottom items are on the right of the toolbar.

**7** If you want to start all over again, click the Reset button.

**8** Click the Close button when you're finished customizing the toolbar.

The toolbar now sports a new Favorites icon, and the Move To and Copy To icons are gone.

**customize folders and windows**

# sort & organize files

The View menu of a folder window lists five different ways to see the file and folder icons inside. Thumbnails gives you the largest icons, followed by Tiles and then Icons. List and Details give you the smallest icons. In any of these views, you can sort the content. You'll now sort in a few different ways in different views.

In the Thumbnails, Tiles, and Icons views, you can move icons around. To get them back in a sorted order go to the View menu, move the mouse to Arrange Icons by, and click on a sorting criteria. Here we'll use Name to sort alphabetically.

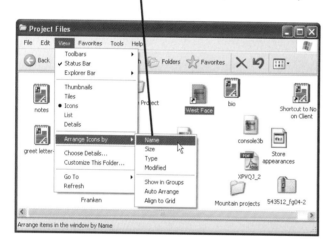

The icons are now sorted alphabetically; folders first, then files.

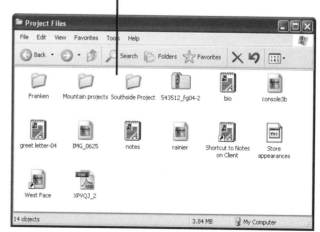

**customize folders and windows**

You'll notice that one of the choices for sorting was Modified. This is short for date modified. This can be a useful way to sort files, though it is more useful in Details view than in icon view.

**1** Go to the View menu and select Details to bring the Details view forward.

**2** The Details view defaults to alphabetical order, again with folders first, then files. You can sort by a particular criterion by clicking on its column head. To sort by date, click the Date Modified column head.

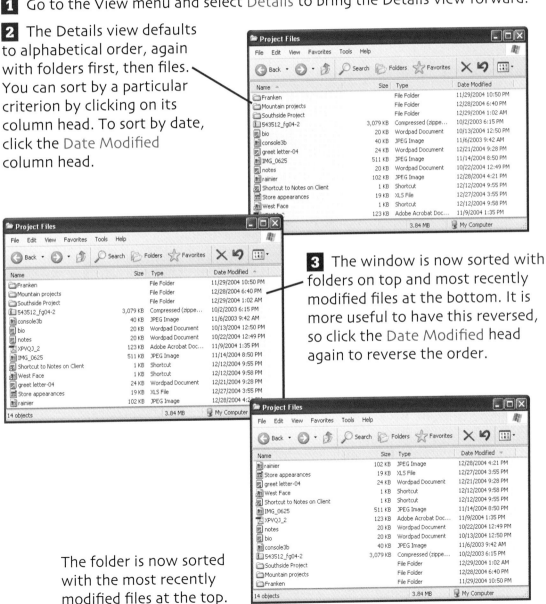

**3** The window is now sorted with folders on top and most recently modified files at the bottom. It is more useful to have this reversed, so click the Date Modified head again to reverse the order.

The folder is now sorted with the most recently modified files at the top.

# modify details view

You can add more sorting criteria to the Details view by displaying more details. One way to do this is to select Choose Details from the View menu, make your selections in the Choose Details dialog box, then click OK. There is, however, an easier way—the shortcut menu.

**1** Right click on any of the column headings.

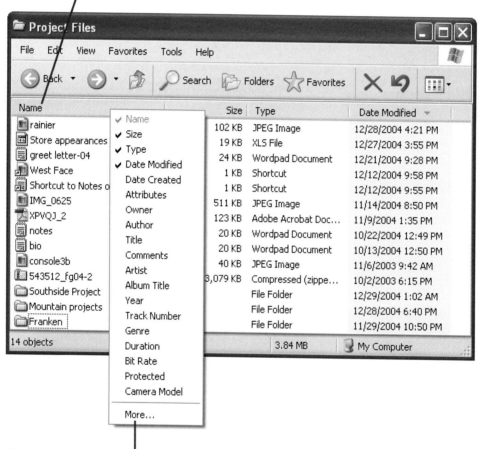

**2** A shortcut menu appears with a list of possible column headings. The criteria that are currently displayed have checkmarks next to them. Clicking one of these to remove the checkmark would hide that column from the window. Here, however, you're going to click Date Created to add it to the window.

**customize folders and windows**

**3** Newly added columns always appear on the far right of the window, sometimes out of view. To make room for it, narrow the Name, Size, and Type columns by dragging the line to the right of the column header on the left.

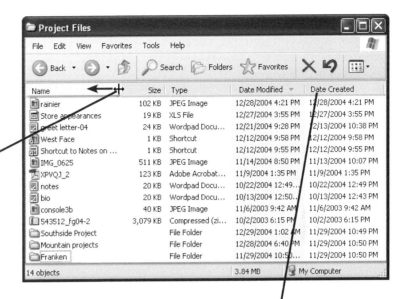

**4** We now want to move the columns around. Grab the Date Created column head and drag it to the left, next to Name.

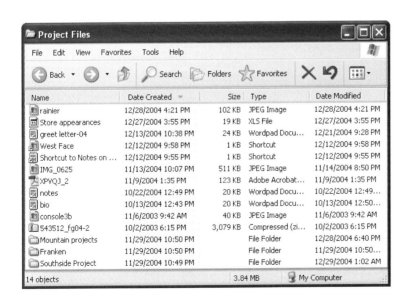

**5** Click Date Created to sort by date. Click again to reverse the sort, putting most recently created files at the top. The result will look like this.

# customize folder icons

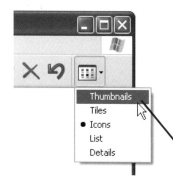

All folder icons don't have to look alike. You can add a picture to a folder icon that Windows will display in Thumbnails view.

**1** Open a window containing the folder you want to customize. If the folder view is not already in thumbnails, click the views icon on the folder toolbar and select Thumbnails.

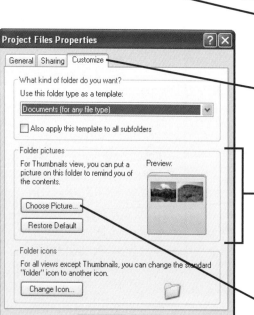

**2** Right-click the folder you want to customize and select Properties.

**3** Click the Customize tab in the properties dialog box.

The middle of the dialog box is a section called Folder pictures. If the current folder contains image files, the sample folder will display up to two of them. If not, this area will be blank.

**4** Click the Choose Picture button.

**customize folders and windows**

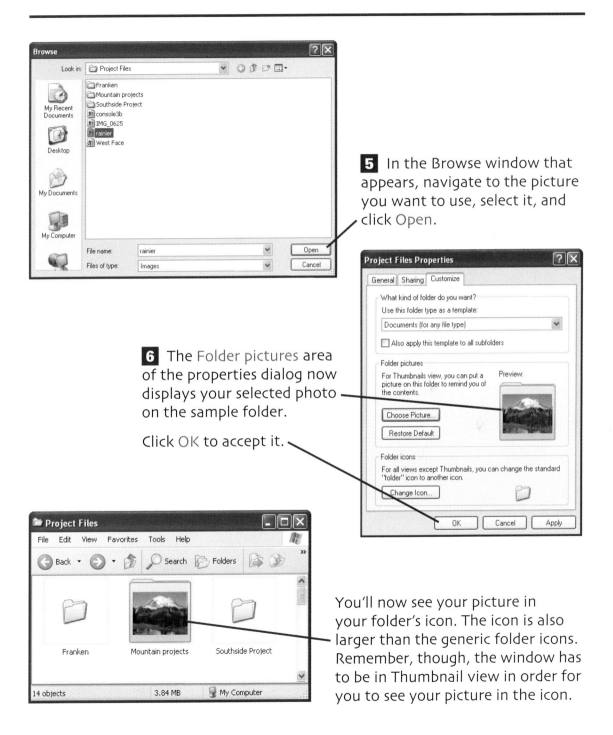

**5** In the Browse window that appears, navigate to the picture you want to use, select it, and click Open.

**6** The Folder pictures area of the properties dialog now displays your selected photo on the sample folder.

Click OK to accept it.

You'll now see your picture in your folder's icon. The icon is also larger than the generic folder icons. Remember, though, the window has to be in Thumbnail view in order for you to see your picture in the icon.

**customize folders and windows**

# replace a folder icon

For other views, you can make a folder stand out by replacing its generic icon with one of dozens of special icons supplied by Windows.

**1** Right-click the folder you want to customize and select Properties. Then choose the Customize tab.

**Southside Project Properties** ？ X

General | Sharing | Customize

What kind of folder do you want?
Use this folder type as a template:

Documents (for any file type) ⌄

☐ Also apply this template to all subfolders

Folder pictures

For Thumbnails view, you can put a picture on this folder to remind you of the contents.

Preview:

[ Choose Picture... ]
[ Restore Default ]

Folder icons

For all views except Thumbnails, you can change the standard "folder" icon to another icon.

[ Change Icon... ]

[ OK ] [ Cancel ] [ Apply ]

**2** Click the Change Icon button at the bottom of the properties dialog box.

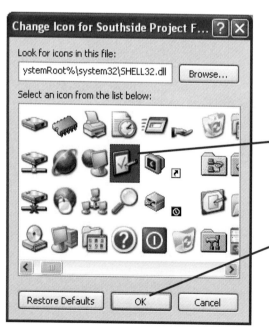

**Change Icon for Southside Project F...** ？ X

Look for icons in this file:

[ ystemRoot%\system32\SHELL32.dll ] [ Browse... ]

Select an icon from the list below:

[ Restore Defaults ] [ OK ] [ Cancel ]

**3** Scroll through the icons; when you find one you like, click to select it.

**4** Click OK to close the icons dialog box.

**customize folders and windows**

**5** Click OK to close the Properties dialog box.

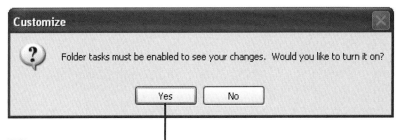

**6** You may get a dialog asking if you would like to turn on Folder Tasks. Click Yes.

Your folder now sports the new icon.

# extra bits

## sort & organize files p. 66

- In addition to sorting, you can organize files by renaming them in a more orderly way. For instance, if the files all start with the same characters, they'll be easier to scan when sorted by name, for example: Murry Analysis, Murry Analysis (1), Murry Analysis (2), etc.. Windows gives you an easy way to rename a group of files with the same name followed by a number.

  Select the files that you want to rename. Right-click one of the selected files and select Rename from the shortcut menu.

  Now type a name for the group of files. Hit Enter, and the files will be renamed.

## customize folder icons p. 70

- If Windows' extra folder icons don't excite you, you can add more. Pear Software's Folder Icon XP (http://www.pear-viewer. com/) is a $20 utility that gives you thousands of great-looking icons to choose for your folders. It's easy to use, too.

# 7. install software and features

In some respects, adding and removing software and software features is the ultimate act of customization you can do to your computer. In this chapter, you'll install programs as well as software features of Windows XP itself. You'll also tell Windows which of these you want to be the default programs.

You'll do most of this in the Add or Remove Programs dialog box.

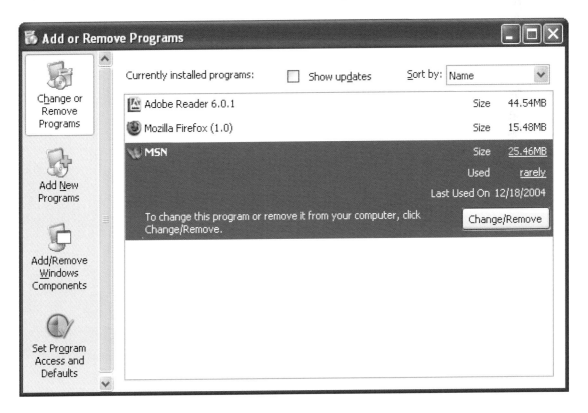

# install a program

You can install a program you download from the Internet or from a CD. In either case, there is usually an installer program called setup.exe or install.exe that is run. Sometimes this is run in the background, and you don't have to do anything. Just download the software or insert the CD, and the installer program takes over. With some programs, you'll see a dialog asking you to install it only after you choose the program from the Start menu.

For other programs, you may insert a CD and nothing will happen. When this occurs, you can tell Windows to install the program.

**1** Go to the Start menu and choose Control Panel.

**2** Double-click the Add or Remove Programs icon.

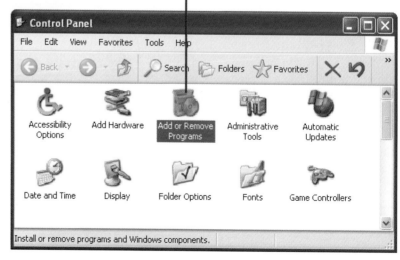

**install software and features**

**3** A dialog appears showing programs you've previously installed. Click the Add New Programs button.

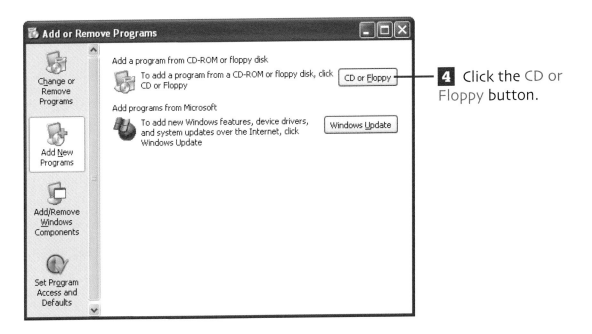

**4** Click the CD or Floppy button.

# install a program (cont.)

**5** Insert the program's installation CD and click the Next button.

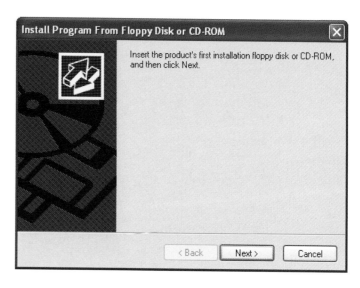

**6** At this point, a dialog box called Run Installation Program will appear.

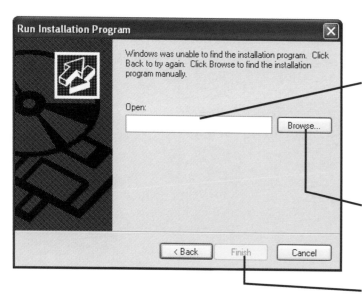

If Windows found the installation program on the CD, it will list it here (something like D:\SETUP.EXE), and you can click the Finish button.

If Windows can't find the installation program, as is the case here, click the Browse button to locate the installer program on the CD.

After you find it and it is listed in the Open field, click Finish.

**install software and features**

# set default program

Windows XP designates certain programs to be the default program.

There are two types of default programs. The first type of default program is related to the Internet: your email, Web browser, instant messaging, and music/video player. The other type of default program is the program that opens when you double-click a certain type of document file.

Often when you install a new program it will ask you if you want it to become the default. If it doesn't, or if you said no, you can still tell Windows XP that you want it to be the default.

First, we'll assign Firefox as the default Web browser. (Firefox is a free Web browser you can download from http://www.mozilla.org.)

**1** Go to the Start menu and choose Control Panel.

**2** In the Control Panel, double-click the Add or Remove Programs icon.

**3** A dialog appears showing programs you've previously installed.

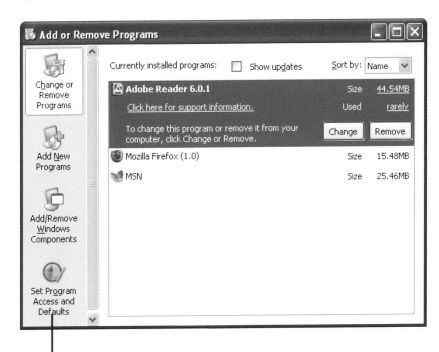

Click the Set Program Access and Defaults button.

# set default program (cont.)

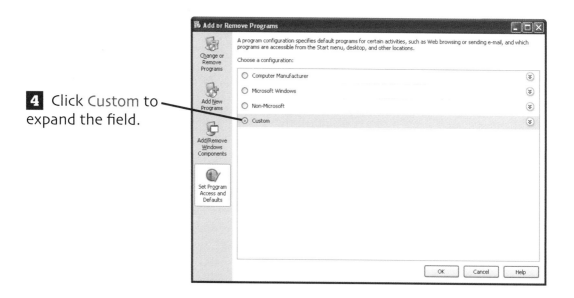

**4** Click Custom to expand the field.

**5** Under each listed category, the dialog box will list the programs that are installed on your computer. In this example, select Mozilla Firefox under the Web browser category.

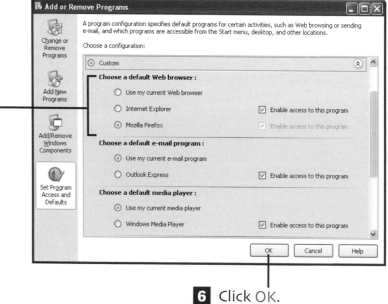

**6** Click OK.

Internet Explorer is still available to you if you want to use it. However, when Windows or another program calls for a Web browser, Firefox will launch.

**install software and features**

# reset a file opener

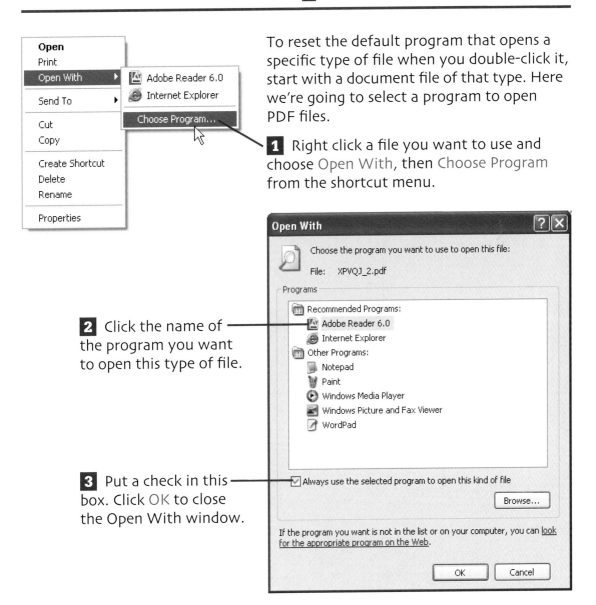

To reset the default program that opens a specific type of file when you double-click it, start with a document file of that type. Here we're going to select a program to open PDF files.

**1** Right click a file you want to use and choose Open With, then Choose Program from the shortcut menu.

**2** Click the name of the program you want to open this type of file.

**3** Put a check in this box. Click OK to close the Open With window.

The next time you double-click this type of file, the program you specified will launch and open the file.

# add/remove features

Whether Windows XP came pre-installed on your PC or you installed it yourself, there are features that may not be installed. Windows calls these extra features components.

There may also be components installed that you aren't using. For instance, if you don't subscribe to Microsoft's MSN Internet services, then you don't need MSN Explorer.

You can easily add new components or remove components you aren't using.

**1** Go to the Start menu and choose Control Panel.

**2** Double-click the Add or Remove Programs icon.

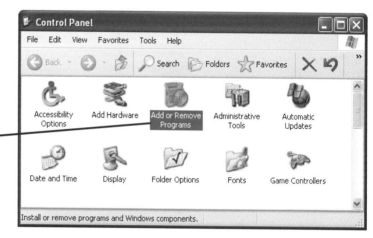

**3** A dialog appears listing the programs and updates that are installed. Click Add/Remove Windows Components to bring up the Windows Component Wizard.

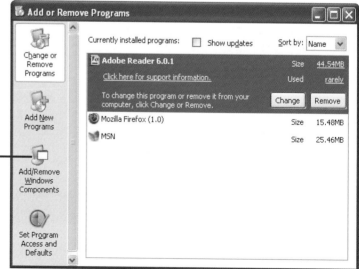

**install software and features**

**4** Put a check next to the feature you want to add. (Or uncheck an item you wish to remove.)

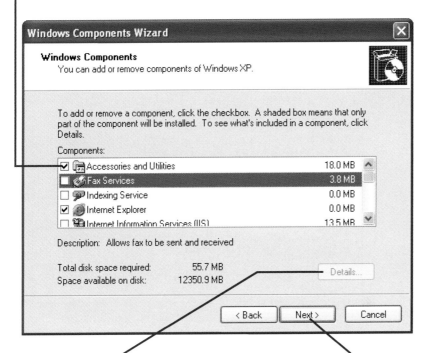

**5** If the Details button is available, that means that the item selected contains subcomponents that you can add or remove separately. You do this by clicking the Details button and checking or unchecking items from a list. If the Details button is grayed out (as it is here), the selected item does not contain subcomponents.

**6** Click the Next button.

**7** Wait while Windows does the installation (or the removal), and then click Finish. If you are installing a component, Windows may ask you to insert your Windows XP CD depending on how your computer is set up and what you are installing.

**install software and features**

# update windows xp

Microsoft regularly releases updates to Windows XP that fix problems and add security from Internet intruders. By default, Windows XP is set to update automatically at 3 am. If you don't have your computer on and connected to the Internet at the time, it won't update. However, you can update any time, as long as you're connected to the Internet.

**1** Go to the Start menu and choose Control Panel.

**2** Double-click the Add or Remove Programs icon.

**3** Click Add New Programs.

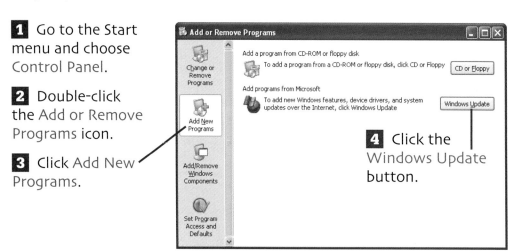

**4** Click the Windows Update button.

**5** Your web browser will launch and connect to a Microsoft Web site. Click Express Install.

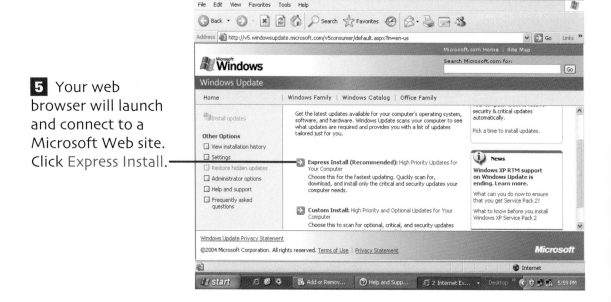

**install software and features**

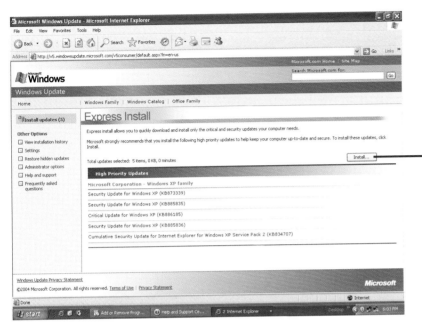

**6** After a few minutes you'll see a list of updates that are not installed on your computer. Click the Install button.

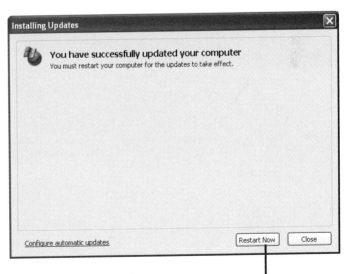

**7** Wait for installation. Click the Restart Now button.

Your computer will restart.

**install software and features**

# extra bits

## install a program p. 76

- Some software programs require you to have a certain version of Windows or a service pack installed on your computer. Fortunately, this kind of technical information is available at your fingertips.

  Open My Computer and select About Windows under the Help menu. A dialog box will display the Windows version and build number and service pack installed.

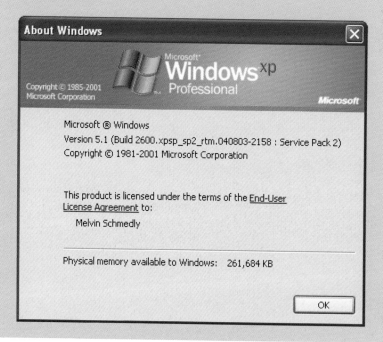

# 8. customize internet access

Most people who use a computer also use the Internet. Windows XP offers many ways to set up Internet access so that it works the way you want it to.

This chapter contains assorted tips for accessing the Internet. You'll set up a high-speed Internet connection, customize aspects of sending and receiving email, and make it easier to access Web sites.

# create a connection

To create an Internet connection, we'll use Windows XP's New Connection Wizard. Be sure you have the account information given to you by your Internet service provider at hand. Creating a dial-up connection is easy, but creating a high-speed connection, such as DSL or cable modem, is much less obvious; windows refers to DSL as a broadband modem connection.

Here you'll create the most common type of DSL connection, one that requires a username and password.

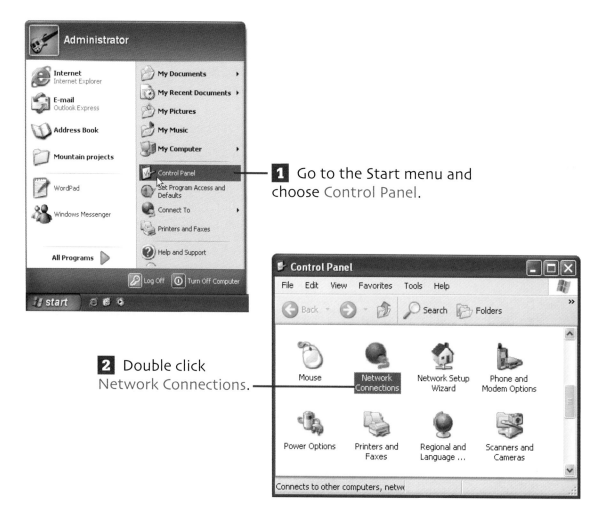

**1** Go to the Start menu and choose Control Panel.

**2** Double click Network Connections.

**customize internet access**

**3** Under Network Tasks, click Create a New Connection.

The New Connection Wizard will appear.

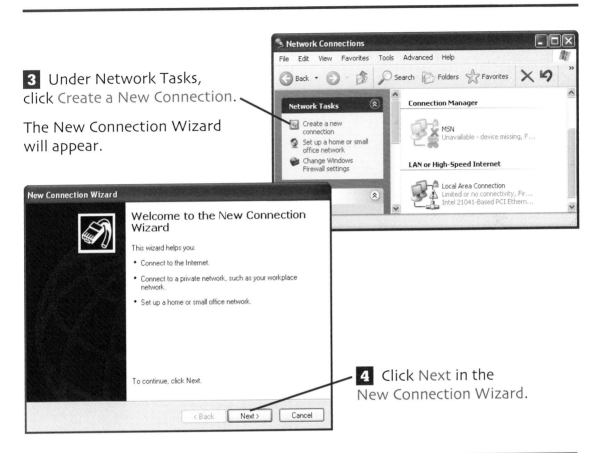

**4** Click Next in the New Connection Wizard.

**5** Select Connect to the Internet.

**6** Click Next.

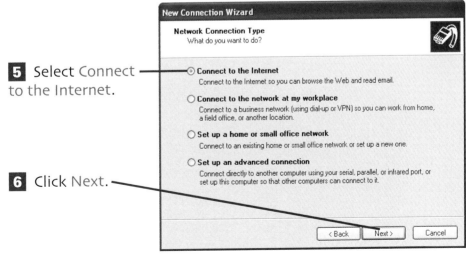

# create a connection (cont.)

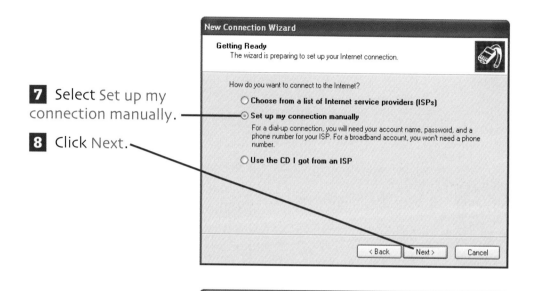

**7** Select Set up my connection manually.

**8** Click Next.

*New Connection Wizard*

**Getting Ready**
The wizard is preparing to set up your Internet connection.

How do you want to connect to the Internet?

○ **Choose from a list of Internet service providers (ISPs)**

◉ **Set up my connection manually**
For a dial-up connection, you will need your account name, password, and a phone number for your ISP. For a broadband account, you won't need a phone number.

○ **Use the CD I got from an ISP**

< Back | Next > | Cancel

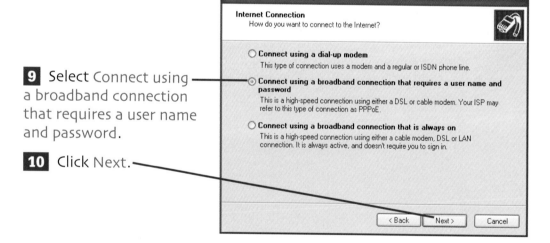

**9** Select Connect using a broadband connection that requires a user name and password.

**10** Click Next.

*New Connection Wizard*

**Internet Connection**
How do you want to connect to the Internet?

○ **Connect using a dial-up modem**
This type of connection uses a modem and a regular or ISDN phone line.

◉ **Connect using a broadband connection that requires a user name and password**
This is a high-speed connection using either a DSL or cable modem. Your ISP may refer to this type of connection as PPPoE.

○ **Connect using a broadband connection that is always on**
This is a high-speed connection using either a cable modem, DSL or LAN connection. It is always active, and doesn't require you to sign in.

< Back | Next > | Cancel

**11** In the next few screens that appear, type in your account information from your Internet service provider. Click Next after each dialog box, and click Finish in the last dialog.

When you click Finish, the wizard disappears and your Internet connection is complete. You're now ready to hook up to the Internet.

**customize internet access**

# connect to the net

When it comes to connecting to the Internet, it doesn't matter if you're using a dialup modem, DSL, or cable modem. The procedure is the same. You begin with the Start menu.

**1** Open the Start menu, click Connect To, and select the name of the connection you set up.

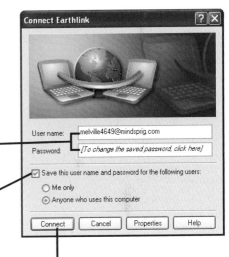

**2** A Connect window opens. Your user name and password should be automatically entered. If not, type them in here.

**3** If you always want your account information automatically entered, make sure the box is checked next to Save this user name and password for the following users.

**4** Click the Connect button.

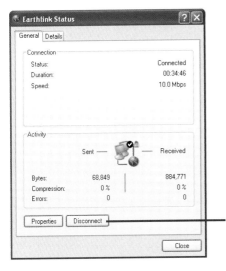

**5** A Status window replaces the Connect window; you're now connected to the Internet. You can browse the web and check email. To close the Internet connection, click the Disconnect button.

# add outlook accounts

In Outlook Express, a wizard launches and asks you for your email account information. If you give the wizard everything it needs, it will set up the connection for you. You can also add a second email account in Outlook Express. This could be for your work email address on a home computer, or an email account for another person.

**1** Open Outlook Express and choose Accounts from the Tools menu.

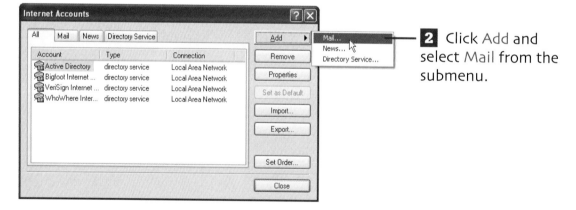

**2** Click Add and select Mail from the submenu.

**3** The Internet Connection Wizard appears, just as it did the first time you opened Outlook Express. In each screen, enter information about your email account from your Internet service provider. Click the Next button to move to the next screen. The last wizard screen has a Finish button. Click it and your email account is ready to use.

**customize internet access**

# turn off email graphics

One of the best customization features in Outlook Express is to turn off graphics in email messages that you receive. Not only will you no longer have to see pictures from advertising that you didn't ask for, but you can prevent spammers from verifying your email address.

When you open an email message from a spammer, your email software tells the spammer's server to send you the picture, which notifies the spammer that your email address is valid. Turn the graphics off, and your email software will not try to contact the spammer.

**1** Go to the Start menu and open Outlook Express.

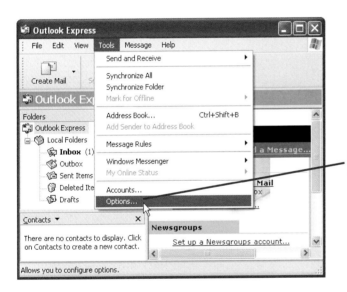

**2** Choose Options from the Tools menu.

**3** In the Options dialog box click the Security tab.

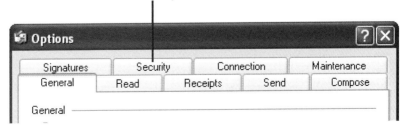

# turn off email graphics

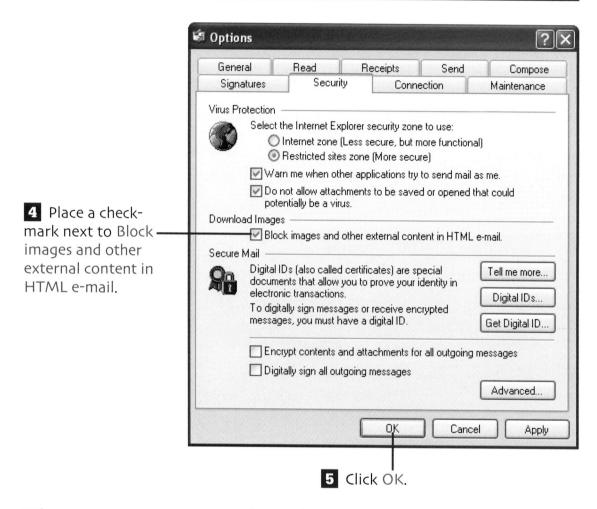

**4** Place a check-mark next to Block images and other external content in HTML e-mail.

**5** Click OK.

When you receive messages, Outlook will tell you if it has blocked pictures. If the message is from someone you know, you can click a link in the email message called Click here to download pictures.

**customize internet access**

# create email groups

If you frequently send email to the same group of people, you can save yourself a lot of typing by creating a list of these addresses, known as a group. You can then send a message to everyone in the group simply by typing the name of the group. Here's how to create a group in Outlook Express.

**1** Click the Addresses icon.

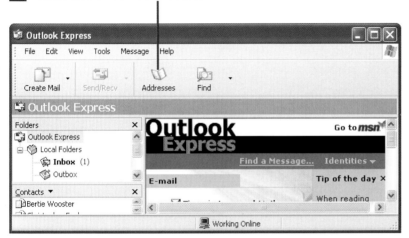

**2** Click and hold the New button and choose New Group from the menu.

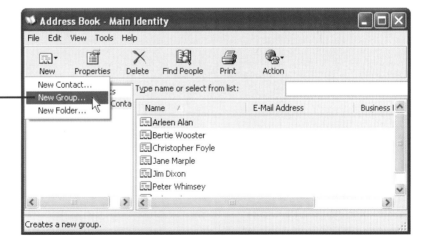

# create email groups (cont.)

**3** Type a group name here.

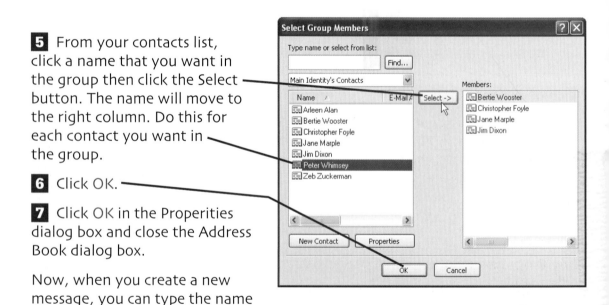

**4** Click the Select Members button.

**5** From your contacts list, click a name that you want in the group then click the Select button. The name will move to the right column. Do this for each contact you want in the group.

**6** Click OK.

**7** Click OK in the Properities dialog box and close the Address Book dialog box.

Now, when you create a new message, you can type the name of the group, in this case Book Club, in the To field. After you send the message, if you look at the message in the Sent Items folder, you'll find each group member listed.

# add links toolbar

The Links toolbar is an area on the Taskbar that contains icons representing Web pages. Click an icon there, and your browser opens to its Web page.

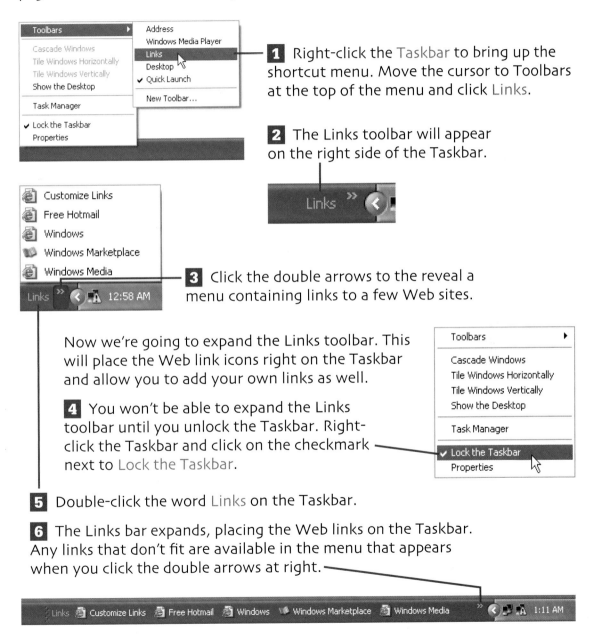

**1** Right-click the Taskbar to bring up the shortcut menu. Move the cursor to Toolbars at the top of the menu and click Links.

**2** The Links toolbar will appear on the right side of the Taskbar.

**3** Click the double arrows to the reveal a menu containing links to a few Web sites.

Now we're going to expand the Links toolbar. This will place the Web link icons right on the Taskbar and allow you to add your own links as well.

**4** You won't be able to expand the Links toolbar until you unlock the Taskbar. Right-click the Taskbar and click on the checkmark next to Lock the Taskbar.

**5** Double-click the word Links on the Taskbar.

**6** The Links bar expands, placing the Web links on the Taskbar. Any links that don't fit are available in the menu that appears when you click the double arrows at right.

# add a link

Now that you have the Links toolbar spread out on the Taskbar, you'll want to add your own Web links. Here, we'll add a Web link and do some editing of the Links toolbar to make it more convenient to access your new link.

**1** Drag your Web link icon from the Address field of your Web browser to the Links toolbar. You can also drag any link on a Web page to the Links toolbar.

**2** Here you don't see the new link on the Taskbar because there isn't room. Instead, if you click the double arrows, you'll find it in the menu.

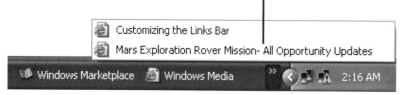

**customize internet access**

**3** To make room on the Taskbar for your new link, grab the top of the Taskbar and drag it upwards.

**4** The Taskbar is now tall enough to fit all of the Web link icons. Now you need to shorten the name of your new link.

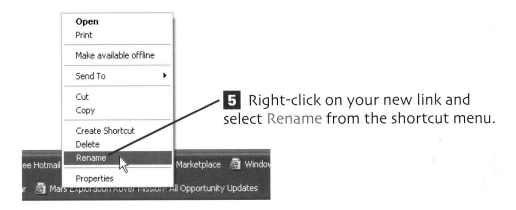

**5** Right-click on your new link and select Rename from the shortcut menu.

**6** Type the new name of the Web link in the Rename dialog box.

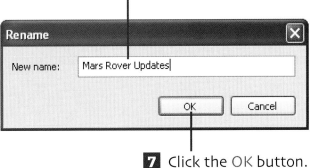

**7** Click the OK button.

# add a link (cont.)

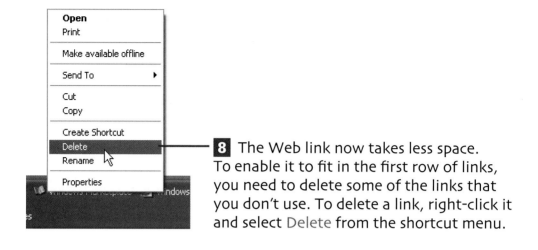

**8** The Web link now takes less space. To enable it to fit in the first row of links, you need to delete some of the links that you don't use. To delete a link, right-click it and select Delete from the shortcut menu.

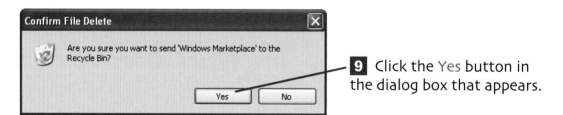

**9** Click the Yes button in the dialog box that appears.

**10** Finally, drag the Taskbar back down to its original size, with your new link visible.

You can lock the Taskbar if you wish by right-clicking an empty space on the Taskbar and choosing Lock the Taskbar.

**customize internet access**

# add address toolbar

The Address toolbar can give you quick access to your favorite Web sites by providing a field where you can type a Web address—directly from the Taskbar.

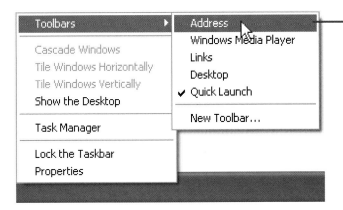

**1** Right-click the Taskbar to bring up the shortcut menu. Choose Toolbars at the top of the menu and then click Address.

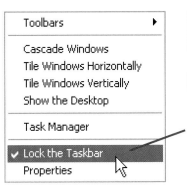

**2** The Address toolbar will appear on the right side of the Taskbar.

**3** You won't be able to open the Address toolbar until you unlock the Taskbar. Right-click the Taskbar and select Lock the Taskbar to remove its checkmark.

# add address toolbar (cont.)

**4** Double-click the word Address on the Taskbar.

**5** The Address bar opens. You can now type in a Web address.

**6** Click the Go button. Your Web browser will open to the Web page you specified.

**7** The Address toolbar remembers the last few Web addresses you typed into it. To see them, click the down arrow on the Address toolbar.

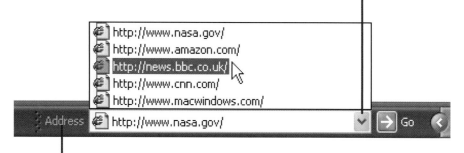

You can double-click the word Address on the Taskbar to close the Address toolbar. If you'd like to keep it open, you can lock the Taskbar by repeating step 3 on the previous page.

# extra bits

## create a connection p. 88

- If you have a constant Internet connection that a DSL or cable modem gives you, your computer will automatically update the time by connecting to a time server on the Internet.

  The automatic time updating may not occur with a dial-up modem connection, but you can manually update the time once you are connected.

  Double-click the time display on the right side of the Taskbar to open the Date and Time Properties dialog box.

  Click the Internet Time tab and place a checkmark next to Automatically synchronize with an Internet time server.

  Click Update Now. Windows will contact the time server and set the correct time on your computer. Click OK to close the dialog box.

## connect to the net p. 91

- You may have noticed that the Internet status window doesn't have a minimize button. Fortunately, you don't need to keep it open while you're logged in to the Internet—you may close it at any time. If you need to bring it up again, go to the right side of the Taskbar and click the double-computer icon. This will open the Internet status window.

## add address toolbar p. 101

- You can use the Address toolbar to access files and folders on your hard drive. Type a path to open the file or folder.

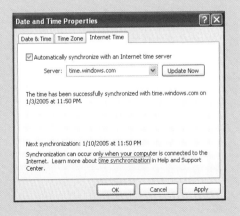

# 9. customize hardware

Got mouse? Of course you do. One way to customize a mouse would be to paint racing stripes on it. A better way is to tweak how Windows interacts with the mouse so that it performs better for you. The other piece of hardware that is just about as common as a mouse is a printer.

In this chapter, you'll learn how to customize your mouse settings and what to do if Windows doesn't recognize your printer after you plug it in.

The starting place for fiddling with hardware settings in Windows XP is the Control Panel.

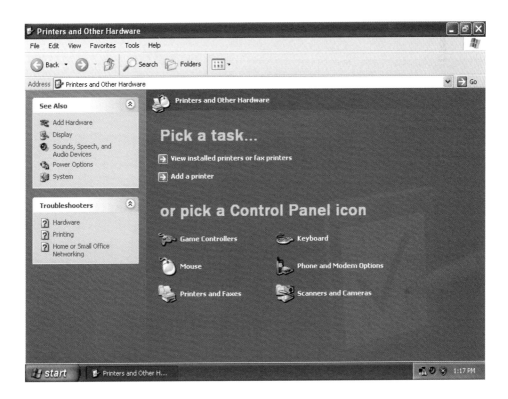

# adjust mouse clicking

The computer mouse is the most personal of your PC's peripherals. Mice come in different sizes and shapes in order to fit different sized hands. But it's also true that not everyone clicks and drags at the same speed. You can change the way the mouse feels by adjusting the clicking and dragging behavior in Windows.

First, you'll adjust how fast you need to double-click your mouse to open a file or folder.

**1** Go to the Start menu and select Control Panel.

**2** In the left side panel, click Switch to Classic View if the Control Panel is not already in Classic mode.

The Control Panel's classic view shows each settings dialog box as an individual icon.

**3** Double-click the Mouse icon.

**customize hardware**

**4** The Mouse Properties window opens with the Buttons tab selected. Try dragging the Speed slider. Dragging to the left will allow a slower double-click to open a folder or file. Sliding it to the right requires a faster double-click.

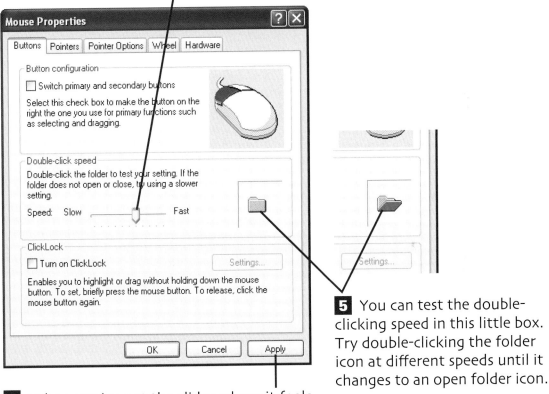

**5** You can test the double-clicking speed in this little box. Try double-clicking the folder icon at different speeds until it changes to an open folder icon.

**6** When you've got the slider where it feels the best, click the Apply button.

# adjust mouse speed

Now we'll adjust the speed of the mouse pointer itself as it moves across the screen.

**1** Click the Pointer Options tab.

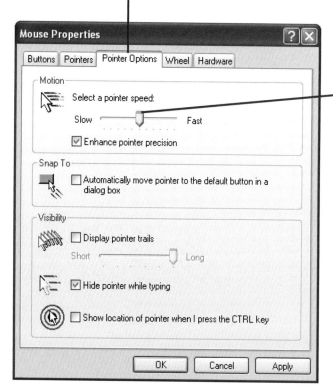

**2** Under Select a pointer speed, drag the slider bar left or right. Move the mouse around to see how the change feels.

Moving the pointer toward Fast will make the mouse pointer move a long distance across the screen with small movements of the mouse. A faster setting is useful if you don't have a lot of desk space on which to navigate the mouse.

Moving the pointer toward Slow will shorten the distance the pointer travels on screen as you move the mouse. A slower setting is useful if you feel you are overshooting objects on screen.

When you have found an adjustment that feels the most comfortable, click the OK button to close the Mouse Properties window.

**customize hardware**

# set up a printer

If Windows XP doesn't recognize your printer when you connect it to your computer, you may have to change some settings to get it working. If a CD came with your printer, run the installer program. If the printer still doesn't work, or you don't have an installer CD, you can run the Add Printer Wizard.

**1** Turn on your printer.

**2** Go to the Start menu, choose Control Panel.
Switch to classic view if not already there.

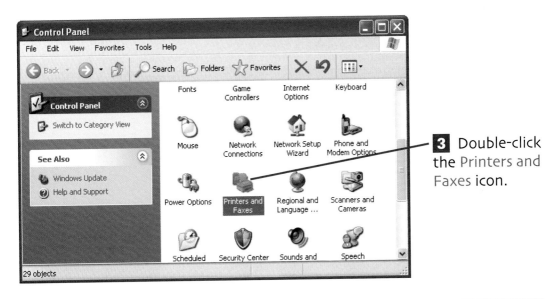

**3** Double-click the Printers and Faxes icon.

**4** Click Add a printer.

# set up a printer (cont.)

**5** The Add Printer Wizard will launch, offering advice and asking questions. When you get to this screen, make sure these two items are checked.

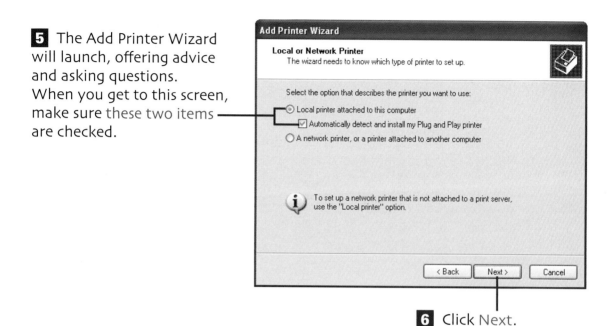

**6** Click Next.

**7** If Windows finds your printer, then you're set. If a window appears telling you it didn't find the printer, click the Next button, which will bring up the Select a Printer Port screen.

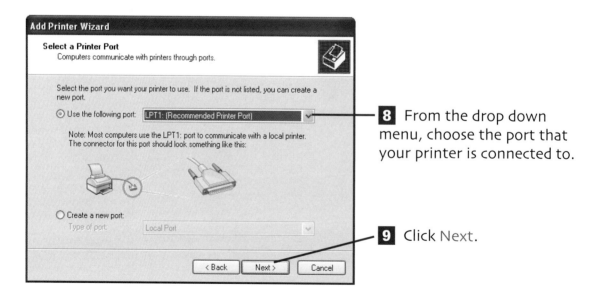

**8** From the drop down menu, choose the port that your printer is connected to.

**9** Click Next.

**customize hardware**

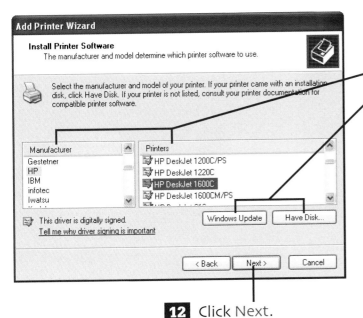

**10** The wizard now asks you for your printer manufacturer and model. Select them from the lists.

**11** If you've download installation files from the Internet, or have a disk, click the Have Disk button. If you have files, click the Browse button that will appear to locate them. Or, click Windows Update to download printer's installation files automatically.

**12** Click Next.

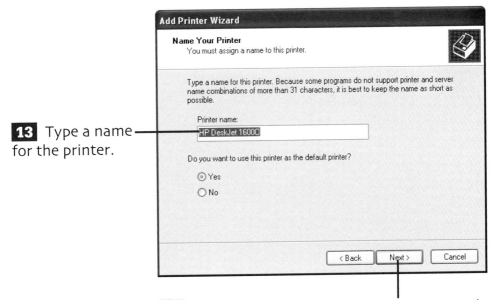

**13** Type a name for the printer.

**14** Click Next, and answer the questions on the next few screens. Click Finish at the last screen.

# extra bits

## adjust mouse speed p. 108

- If you have a mouse with a scroll wheel, you can adjust the speed of scrolling. Click the Wheel tab of Mouse Properties dialog box to get to the settings.

## set up a printer p. 109

- If you have some other piece of hardware connected to your computer that Windows isn't recognizing, try running the Add Hardware Wizard. With the Control Panel in classic view, double-click Add Hardware. Click through the Wizard's screens and choose the type of device.

  If the wizard detects the hardware device, double-click it to see if the wizard offers any advice. Then complete the wizard with the Next and Finish buttons.

  If the wizard doesn't detect your device, click Search for and Install the Hardware Automatically. In the next screen, choose the manufacturer and model of the device. If you have a disk or files that you downloaded for the device, click the Have Disk button. For files, use the Browse button to locate them. Finally, complete the wizard.

  If you still can't get a printer working, open the Printers and Faxes icon in Control Panel and click Troubleshoot Printing in the left column. A dialog box will appear asking you questions about your problem and offer suggestions on how to fix it.

**customize hardware**

# 10. set up multiple users

So now you've gone through this book, fiddled with various settings in different parts of your computer, and adapted Windows XP to just the way you want it to look and act.

Then your spouse comes along and finds that things don't look the way they're supposed to. Worse yet, your kids get at your PC and do their own customization that is beyond your recognition.

It's time to give each person who uses the PC his or her own user account. Each user can then log in to the computer with their own user name and make their own customizations without affecting the way Windows looks to the other users. Each user will have their own individually customized Windows XP.

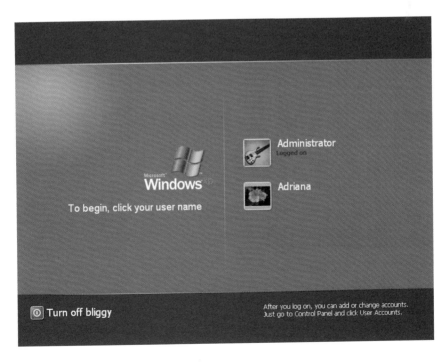

# add a user account

You create user accounts one at a time, each with an individual user name. Here's what to do to create your next user account.

**1** Go to the Start menu and choose Control Panel.

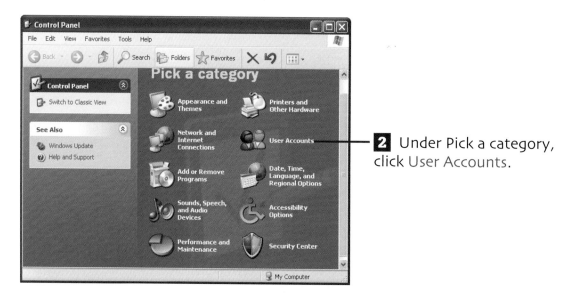

**2** Under Pick a category, click User Accounts.

**3** Under Pick a task click Create a new account.

**set up multiple users**

**4** Type in a name for the account.
A person's first name works just fine.

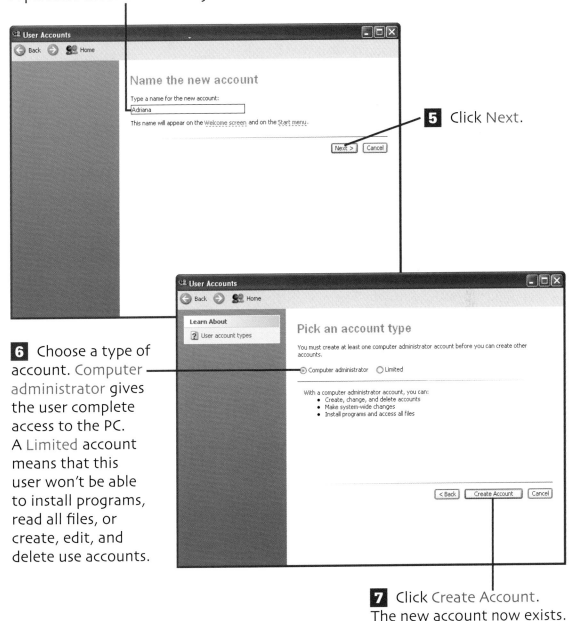

**5** Click Next.

**6** Choose a type of account. Computer administrator gives the user complete access to the PC. A Limited account means that this user won't be able to install programs, read all files, or create, edit, and delete use accounts.

**7** Click Create Account.
The new account now exists.

# add a user password

After you create a new user account, the main User Accounts window reappears displaying it. Initially, the new account has the same icon as your account and has no password for log in. A password isn't necessary, but if you want the user to have one, here's how to create it.

**1** Click the new user name.

**2** A new screen appears giving you some options to change. Click Create a password.

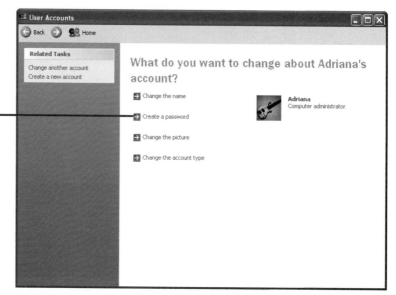

**set up multiple users**

The next screen appears with a warning that the user will lose stored passwords and other info. If this is a brand new user account, there won't be any information to lose.

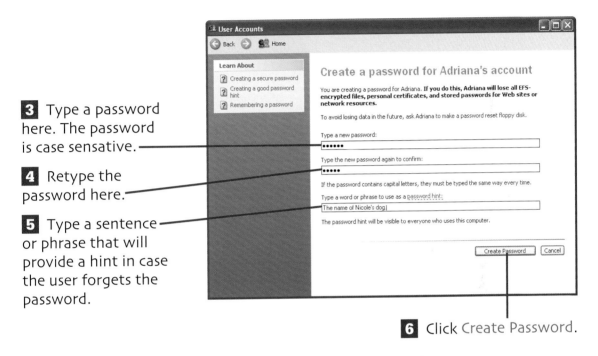

**3** Type a password here. The password is case sensative.

**4** Retype the password here.

**5** Type a sentence or phrase that will provide a hint in case the user forgets the password.

**6** Click Create Password.

The screen from step 2 reappears asking you what you want to change. Let's change the user icon this time.

# change the user icon

Now that you're back at the main User Accounts dialog box, lets assign a new icon to the user account.

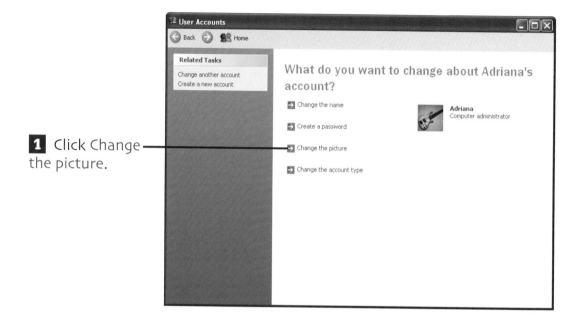

**1** Click Change the picture.

**2** Choose a picture from the selection Windows provides or use an image of your own. To use your own image, click Browse for more pictures.

x

**set up multiple users**

**3** A window opens to My Pictures. Find the picture you want to use and click to select it, or navigate to the picture in another location.

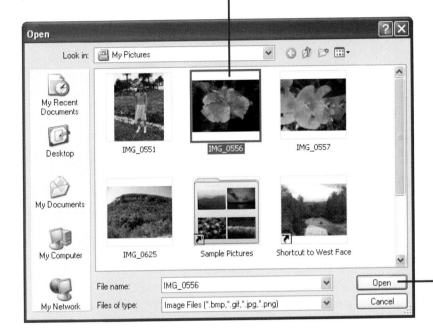

**4** Click Open.

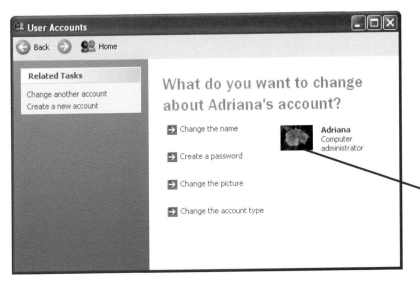

Back in the User Accounts dialog box, you'll now see your picture as the user icon. Close this window by clicking the X box in the upper right.

**set up multiple users**

# switch between users

Windows XP allows you to switch between users at any time without having to close your programs. This enables another user to log in. Then, when you log back in, you'll find everything right where you left it.

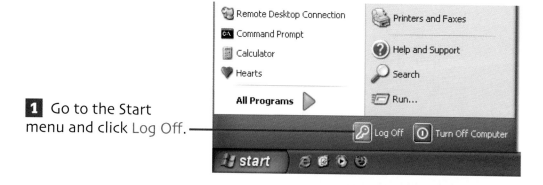

**1** Go to the Start menu and click Log Off.

**2** In the Log Off Windows dialog, click the Switch User button.

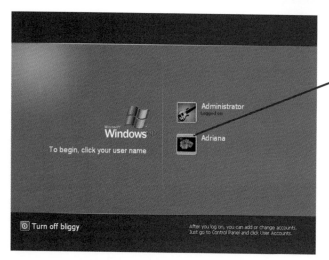

**3** A screen appears showing all of the user accounts set up on the computer. Click the account button for the new user you set up.

Windows XP will now launch for the new user, bringing up a completely standard Desktop, Start menu, Taskbar, and other interface elements and basic programs.

**set up multiple users**

# extra bits

**switch between users** p. 120

- The reason you can switch from one user to another without closing your programs is that a feature called fast user switching is turned on by default when you create new user accounts. This works great for a home or small office PC. However, if you are concerned about security, you can turn off fast user switching, which would require that all programs close and Windows shut down before allowing another user to log on.

- To disable fast user switching, go to the Start menu, click Control Panel, and open the User Accounts category. Now click Change the Way Users Log On and Off. You can now uncheck Use Fast User Switching.

# index

# index

# index

# index

## O

OK button, 8
Open With option, 81
Outlook Express, 92–96
   creating email groups in,
      95–96
   opening, 93
   setting up email accounts in,
      92
   turning off email graphics in,
      93–94

## P

passwords, 113, 116–117
PC World magazine, 22
Pear Software, 74
photos
   adding to folder icons, 70–71
   adding to user-account icons,
      118–119
   displaying resolution of, 22
   replacing Desktop, 10–13, 22
   setting Outlook Express to
      block, 93–94
   for user-account icons,
      118–119
pinning, 42–43, 44
Player, Windows Media, 32–33
Pointer Options tab, 108
pointer speed, 108
printer settings, 109–111, 112
Printers and Faxes icon, 109, 112
Professional, Windows XP, 46
programs
   adding to Start menu, 42–43
   adding to Taskbar, 30–32
   installing, 75–78, 86
   opening, 32, 42
   removing from Start menu,
      45
   setting default, 79–80
   switching users without
      closing, 120, 121
   viewing installed, 80

Properties command, 3
properties dialog boxes, 3, 8

## Q

question mark, 6
Quick Launch toolbar, 30–32, 61

## R

Recent Documents submenu, 46
Remove from This List
   command, 45
Rename command, 74, 99
Reset button, 65
resolution, 14–17, 22
Restart Now button, 85
right-clicking, 2
right-dragging, 48
Run Installation Program dialog
   box, 78

## S

screen resolution, 14–17
scroll wheel, mouse, 112
Security tab, 93
security updates, 84
Select Members button, 96
separators, toolbar, 64–65
service packs, 86
Set Program Access and Defaults
   button, 79
settings dialog boxes, 4
setup.exe, 76, 78
shortcut menus, 2
shortcuts
   creating, 29, 49, 61
   deleting, 52–54
   renaming, 29
Show Text option, 57
Size column head, 69
Slow pointer option, 108

software. See programs
spammers, 93
Speed slider, 107
Start menu, 35–46
   adding folders to, 44
   adding programs to, 42–43
   changing number of
      programs on, 37
   classic vs. standard, 46
   converting links to menus in,
      39–41
   purpose of, 35
   removing items from, 45
   resizing icons in, 36–38
   ways of customizing, 35
Status bar, 62
Support icon, 8
Switch to Classic View option, 4
Switch User button, 120

## T

Taskbar, 23–34
   adding icons to, 55–57
   adding programs to, 30–32
   adding toolbars to, 24–26
   adding Web links to, 97–100
   adding Windows Media
      player to, 32–33
   locking/unlocking, 24, 32,
      34, 55, 100, 101
   moving, 34
   moving toolbars to Desktop
      from, 27
   purpose of, 23
   removing toolbars from, 34
   widening Quick Launch area
      in, 32
themes, 18–21, 22
Themes tab, 18, 22
Thumbnails view, 66, 70
Tiles view, 66
time server, 103